YOU CAN REPLACE THE JERK AT THE TOP

THE JERK AT THE TOP

A GUIDE TO SUCCESS IN CORPORATE AMERICA

ROBERT VINES

ISBN: 978-1-66782-429-1 (printed)

ISBN: 978-1-66782-430-7 (eBook)

Clear and Candid Explanation of the Management World

In my 40-plus years of teaching and research on the college/university level, I don't think I have seen a more clear and candid explanation of the world of management. It is suitable for managers on all levels of an organization because it gives them a lens through which they can see the positives and negatives of decisions made by individuals in all levels of management and how these may affect the overall long-term effectiveness of the organization.

It is also perfect for college students and other individuals studying general management, personnel, or communications so they can better understand how personal decisions can work to the benefit or the detriment of large or small business organizations - must-read for anyone who wants to understand how corporate America really works.

Dr. Richard Bennington

Professor of Business and Home Furnishings (recently retired)

High Point University

High Point, North Carolina

Absolute Gem

Robert's book is an absolute gem. It is filled with good advice, as well as on-point examples. It is well-written and entertaining. Looking back on my own corporate experiences, I can affirm all of his helpful tips and could provide similar examples confirming his conclusions.

The only regret I have about the book is that it wasn't published 50 years ago; I could have used it. Everyone planning to pursue a career in corporate America should read this book. When it is published, I intend to gift this book to all the young sons and daughters of friends who are entering the corporate world.

Kenneth B. Brown Sr.

Retired IBM Executive Division Director

Unhesitatingly Recommend

I just completed reading Robert Vines' book, *"You Can Replace the Jerk at the Top"* and I have to say, I really enjoyed it. I found it very thought-provoking, and it caused me to reflect back on my own forty-plus year career and the similar experiences that I was confronted with. In my case, I was able to navigate through each situation and learn many of the lessons described in this book. Had I read this book earlier in my career, I would have been able to avoid some circumstances and deal better with others. As they say, learning from your own mistakes is a great way to learn but an even better way is to learn from others. With that thought in mind, I can unhesitatingly recommend this book to young or mid-career professionals as a way to accelerate their careers and increase their advancement potential.

Martin DiGirolamo

Director and General Manager

Lexmark International

ABOUT THE AUTHOR

Robert Vines is a middle manager who moved successfully up corporate ladders in 4 Fortune 500 companies, regularly interfacing with top executives. He was a Plant Manager at Lexmark International, the printer spin-off from IBM when he left to do consulting, including assignments for Coopers & Lybrand and IBM specializing in polymer processing and new facilities start-ups. This broad background gave him unique insight into executive effectiveness as well as how top managers navigated the circuitous path to the top.

He is a Distinguished Toastmaster and has been a frequent speaker at universities and technical conferences on Concurrent Engineering, Design for Manufacturability, and Off Shore Sourcing of Manufacturing. In addition, he is an avid environmentalist and has been a Texas Master Naturalist for 10 years and enjoys volunteering in state and local parks.

This book is dedicated to all the bosses who failed in their never-ending quest to fire me.

CONTENTS

Notes to the Reader xiii

In the Beginning... xiv

Preface xvi

Move All Jobs Out of the USA...xviii

1. Find the Right Fit 1

Know Thyself 1

Understand Management Candidate Requirements 4

1.   Have the right education (Life is like a camera...when things don't work out...take
     another shot.)..4

2.   Create a professional résumé and cover letter 5

3.   Look the part 11

4.   Personal life = professional life...14

5.   Develop and protect your credit rating 16

6.   Sleep six to eight hours a night 17

7.   Choose a compatible life partner 17

8.   Learn how to be interviewed 19

9.   Have the courage to say no 20

10. Never stop looking for another job...21

11. Don't let pride interfere with your judgment 24

2. Develop Skills 26

Become a Good Salesman 26

Master Negotiation Techniques 29

Perfect Presentation Skills 30

Understand Body Language and Nonverbal Clues...33

Study the Differences in International Cultures 34

Learn How to Conduct Business in Foreign Countries......................................40

Travel Without Stress 41

3. Do Your Job Well 45

Understand your Company's Business (not just your job) 45

Develop a Passion for Your Job 46

Work Long Hours 48

Stay Squeaky Clean Ethically. 49

Never Ever Be Late 51

Do What You Say and Only Say What You Know 52

Do Well What You Do 54

Take the Initiative 54

Practice "Completed Staff Work" Principals 55

4. Preparing to Move Up 58

Be Visible. 58

Present a Positive Attitude 59

Treat Everyone with Respect (everybody votes) 60

Cultivate Connections 62

The Boss is Always Right 63

Choose Your Boss Wisely 64

Know Your Boss and Try to Meet His Needs 66

Blend with the Politics and Beliefs 67

Relationships Are More Important Than Being Right. 68

Prepare for the Day that Work Ends 69

5. Basic Rules for Managers 71

Obtain Formal Management Training 71

Appraise Employees with Fairness and Sensitivity. 73

Understand all Aspects of Your Area 75

Address Accusations of Misconduct Promptly 76

Avoid Discrimination 78

Cultivate a Few Trusted Critics 81

Never Threaten Employees...84

Tell Employees What is Needed, Not What you Want............................86

Terminate With Cause...87

6. Focus on Employees 90

Find the Right Jobs for Your Employees..90

Make Training a Part of Every Employee's Job...................................92

Hire a Bell Ringer 94

Expect Employees to Be what you Want Them to Be 97

Recognize Accomplishments and Always Credit Effort 99

Discipline Employees with Delicacy and Diplomacy 101

7. Manage with Excellence 103

Delegate Effectively 103

Never Act on Only One Version of a Story..104

Take a Break..105

A Break for You (After reading this far, you need a break yourself.)............106

Be a transparent Manager. 107

Resist One-hour Meetings 108

Manage Your Ego..110

8. Become a Management Professional   112

When you Change Jobs, Do Nothing...112

Occasionally, Create a Crisis 113

Adopt a "Program Du Jour" 115

Budget High 116

Develop and Protect your Suppliers 118

Maintain your Own In-House Experts 120

Try to Consider the "why" Behind the Statement..............................122

Be a "Show Me" and "Why" Manager. 123

Never Make Offhand Comments. 124

Provide an Effective Office Environment 125

9. Make Your Style A Differentiator 128

Pick Up Trash – The world is changed by your example, not by your opinion.
(Paul Coelho) 128

Keep your Feet on the Ground. 130

Sometimes you Will Need to be Simply "A Lot of People" 131

10. Securing the Top 133

Keep your Personal Interest First. 133

Sailing Can be Rewarding. 136

Never Go Around your Boss. 137

Make your Own Presentations 139

Keep your Best People 140

Treat People as Numbers. 141

Be Cautious about Being Honest with Employees. 143

11. Reflect on the Choices 145

Unfortunate Consequences for Managers 145

Jerkitude can Creep Up on you 147

Choices 150

Summary 151

Afterword 153

A Better Way 153

NOTES TO THE READER

So, what's a jerk?

Jerks are people who culpably fail to appreciate the perspectives of the people around them, treating others as tools to be manipulated or fools to be dealt with rather than as moral and epistemic peers. To be a jerk is to be ignorant in a certain way—ignorant of the value of others, ignorant of the merit of their ideas and plans, dismissive of their desires and beliefs, unforgiving of their perceived inferiority. (*The Paris Review*) Or, simply: A jerk is a self-centered person whose actions often harm others in order to achieve personal gain.

In a humorous vein, who can forget comedian Steve Martin's portrayal of a jerk in the 1979 cult classic "The Jerk," written by Carl Reiner. In fact, it was so popular that *The Guardian* named it the 24th best comedy film of all time.

Note: Gender-neutral. As I began writing this book, I found it more logical to simply make the entire book masculine. My "he" is intended to be gender neutral. (Like men, women can also be jerks.) In fact, some of the "he's" in the examples were actually "she's".

IN THE BEGINNING

My first professional job was as an engineer-in-training for a large automotive company. Having no industrial experience, I was gratified to discover that there were several senior employees who were absolutely exceptional at their jobs, always knowing how things should be done for the best interest of the company. They were the "go-to" guys when I needed help or direction. In fact, they were so good at everything I wondered why they had not moved up in the organization long before.

My job also included ferrying visiting executives around the company. That exposed me to many members of the top management. I couldn't help but notice that none of these executives seemed to be in the same class as many of the senior folks I had come to know. Generally, the executives were arrogant and self-centered, often putting their own interests above the interests of the company. In fact, most of them seemed to be real jerks. The big mystery for me was how a jerk could climb to the top rung of a major corporation. As I read about the lives of Henry Ford, Steve Jobs, and many of the other famous top managers, I invariably noticed long histories of inconsiderate and sometimes brutal actions they took to achieve and protect their status and turf in the company. It is easy to see that in many ways, they were bona fide jerks. It was more difficult to understand why.

I came to understand this mystery only after years of observing the actions of others who eventually achieved success in attaining executive positions. Those same years in corporate environments also enabled me to recognize the mistakes I had made personally that stifled my own opportunity for moving to the top of the management ladder. The old saying: "Only a fool learns from his own mistakes", embarrasses me but should inspire you to read further and learn from an "old fool".

PREFACE

This book is a guide for success in a corporate environment. But, of course, "success" can be defined differently, depending on personal goals and aspirations.

Most will define success as ultimately achieving a senior level or even the top job in the company. However, although that definition is certainly the main focus, this book also recognizes that success can be obtaining and maintaining a secure and challenging job for a lifetime career. In today's volatile corporate environment, making it to retirement age without experiencing a period of non-employment can indeed be considered success. Certainly, success can also be simply enjoying a career doing work that results in personal satisfaction and enjoyment. However, if your goal is management excellence and advancement, then this book is for you.

To get to the top of a corporation, you have to perform in a manner that will ensure job security. You also have to perform in a manner that will put you at the top of the list of promotional candidates.

Therefore, regardless of how you define success, you will benefit from understanding what it takes to get to the top of an organization. You will also see why so many who have reached the top positions can occasionally, seem to be real jerks. With luck, you'll even be able to figure out how to achieve similar success and to avoid becoming a jerk.

Management books should be quick and easy to read. With that in mind, I have organized this book such that you can quickly flash through the points that you already agree with, and understand, and simply focus on the points where you have interest. Of course, all the points are valuable and salient life lessons that you can benefit from reading even outside of a corporate structure. (OK, maybe one or two are valuable and salient.) On the other hand, if you are reading this to simply confirm your own observations about an executive you know, who is a jerk, you can skip down to chapter 10, "Securing the Top." Also, you might notice that I have occasionally repeated a point from a previous chapter for those who might be "subject-only" reading.

The tips for getting to the top of a corporation are divided into four sections. Chapters 1-4 help you find the right job, excel in your work, and become a candidate for advancement. Chapters 5-9 give you tips on how to be an effective and superior manager. Chapter 10 includes suggestions for achieving the top job in an organization and staying there. It is also where you find the solution to my "big mystery." Chapter 11 is simply a reflection on the management environment in major corporations to incent ideas that the reader might use to improve processes in their own organization.

I hope that the tips that I have listed will assist those who are currently striving for advancement in a corporate environment. I also hope the insights in these points can also become an epiphany for those who may feel disappointed in their career progress. And I am certain that those in executive positions today will find cause for reflection as they make choices on staffing, promotions, and daily decisions. The tips will also afford some readers information that allows them to simply put their career in perspective because the advice would require personal sacrifice and life changes that they are not willing to make. These tips are also my attempt to express the advice I wish I had had when I was younger. (much, much, younger)

To summarize, managers who get to the top must be dedicated and good at their job. Managers who get to the top must be capable and effective managers. Managers who get to the top will also discover that they sometimes find themselves being a bit of a jerk.

Finally, before starting the logical progression of tips that can help get you to the top, I am inserting one of the typical topics found in the section on actions to consider for reaching the top. I am strategically putting it upfront to give you a flavor of how a top manager could be regarded as something of a jerk. However, Chapter 10 reveals more vivid examples of how self-serving actions may be a requirement for reaching the top. It is those self-serving actions that reflect the level of jerkitude* in a top manager.

Note. I used the term "jerkitude" to embrace the degree of jerkiness necessary to climb to the upper reaches of the organization ladder.

According to the Urban Dictionary, "jerkitude" refers to a jerk's attitude. "Anyone that is acting like a putz, a loser, a loon can be described as jerkitude."

Move All Jobs Out of the USA

You can make lots of money for the stockholders by moving jobs out of the United States.

Early in my career, I helped move jobs from the North to the South. Wages were slightly less in the South, but that was not the motivation. It seems that the labor unions in the North were so strong that they were practically running the company.

One plant I helped move to the South was in Milwaukee. It was afternoon when I first visited the plant. As I walked through the facility, I noticed that the entire factory was all but shut down. Only a few machines were running. Most of the employees were sitting around playing cards on tables made out of stacked shipping pallets. When I asked my host what was going on, he explained that the union employees were only required to meet 100% of the daily production standard. When the workers met the standard, they stopped work. He said that even though most employees had met the standard by 2:00 in the afternoon, they could not clock out until 4:00. The standards were one aspect of the labor contract that the union refused to change.

The next day as I started my first full day working there, they assigned me a desk that had a faulty drawer. I noticed several similar desks sitting in a mezzanine storage area. I went up the stairs to the area, pulled out one of the drawers to swap with the one in my desk, and started back down from the mezzanine. As I was coming down the stairs, I met an hourly employee coming up. He immediately stopped me and said that I was taking his job. I tried to hand him the drawer, but he said it was too late. Later, I learned that he had written a grievance and had been paid four hours of overtime pay to compensate for a non-union person doing manual labor.

Early the second day of working there, I was walking through a machining area and noticed that one of the plastics injection molding machines was slamming shut instead of closing slowly. This was obviously because the low-pressure switch was set too high. I took out my penknife and started to twist the adjustment, but remembering the experience from the day before, I asked the operator to make the change. He said that adjusting a valve was a maintenance function, not an operator function. I told him to please stop the machine and wait until I returned with the maintenance person.

I then went to the maintenance area and did all the paper-work to get a machine repairman to follow me to the molding press. When we got to the molding press, he said that even though it was a hydraulic valve, we needed an electrician to be there because there were wires coming out of the machine. I told him to hold on while I went to get an electrician.

I did the same paperwork and came back with an electri-cian about an hour later. When the electrician looked at the job, he pointed out that we would first have to have a millwright move the conveyor beside the machine because it was not safe for the machine repairman to reach the valve. I then told the three of them to wait until I found a millwright.

After completing the paperwork and returning with the mill-wright, I was informed that three or more maintenance people on one job required a supervisor. So, I went back to maintenance and brought one of the supervisors. When he arrived, he said that we also needed the production supervisor because it involved his area. After I found the production supervisor, the millwright moved the con-veyor, the electrician shut off the power, and the machine repairman turned the screw one-fourth turn, all while two supervisors watched. Fixing that silly machine only took seven hours and seven people instead of one person, two minutes, and a penknife.

That evening I told the plant manager my story of my first two days in his plant and he said, "And you thought we were moving south for lower wages."

It was only a few years after that move that we began mov-ing manufacturing out of the South. We first moved to Mexico and

Japan, and then later China and India. While the labor unions that crippled manufacturing efficiencies in the North were beginning to be a factor in the South, it was not the number one reason for leaving the U.S.

The number one reason for leaving the U.S. was **profit to the stockholders**. How would foreign locations mean profit? If goods are manufactured in the U.S. and sold in the U.S., the profits are taxed at the high rates for corporations. If goods are manufactured outside the U.S. and sold in the U.S., the high **U.S. tax rates** on profits can be avoided. The savings can be achieved by setting up offshore subsidiaries in tax havens like Switzerland. These "headquarters" can act like shell companies, as all the actual direction is coming from the U.S., but they serve the purpose. Profits are now taxed at the minuscule rate of the offshore subsidiary.

Countries often agree to a zero-tax rate for a defined period as an incentive if a company locates a headquarters in their country. For a big company, the difference can be hundreds of millions in added profit. A 2016 *Time* magazine article highlighting this fact, noted that Apple Inc. had avoided $14.5 billion in tax payments under one of these schemes by using an offshore headquarters in Ireland. The story further indicated that companies have accumulated a total of $2.4 trillion in cash by striking country-by-country deals like Apple's.

The second reason for leaving the U.S. is that **government regulations and bureaucracy** make operating in America difficult. For example, according to The Competitive Enterprise Institute, 3,410 new regulations were enacted in 2016 alone. Further, it asserts that compliance overhead is estimated to be costing $1.9 trillion per year. Although these costs certainly reduce competitiveness for U.S. manufacturing, the problem I have struggled with so many times is the delays from the inspection and permitting processes associated with growing companies.

By contrast, when I started moving work to Japan and China, I could hardly believe the difference compared to the US. Their governments seem to be partnering with industry instead of putting up roadblocks. In Mexico, where regulations often mimic the U.S., compliance is often simply a phone call to the "right person" who would expedite inspections. This is not to imply that we didn't meet regulations, we always did. Moreover, our own internal standards and controls exceeded government requirements. It was the bureaucracy that was such a difference.

The advent of **labor unions** moving into the South is reason No. 3 for moving out of the U.S. (which I have already mentioned). The fourth and final reason is **labor costs**. (And you thought it was the only reason.) Labor cost overseas is lower, but for many products, the labor savings aren't sufficient to cover the added costs of shipping and inventory. The six-week ocean shipping delay adds inventory carrying costs in addition to the increased transportation. One simple product I worked on had only $2.07 in assembly costs while in the U.S. Although the assembly costs in China were estimated to be less than $.50, the shipping and inventory carrying costs added another $2.25 to deliver that product to our door. Therefore, moving to China for that product actually represented a cost increase. We moved it to China anyway. After all, there are still reasons one, two, and three.

The tip then, is that if your company still has operations in the U.S., you could be the person to demonstrate the benefits of leaving the country. It's an easy sell if you can get the proposal to top management. If you are in on the ground floor of the move, you might even have a chance of heading the shell operation in Switzerland. Switzerland is a beautiful place to live.

Personally, I worry about all the jobs I helped move out of the U.S. Those moves added up to tens of thousands of jobs, if I include all of the parts suppliers and support services involved in manufacturing that I helped take out of the country. At first, the basic labor jobs are moved, but what follows is always a progression to higher and higher skill levels. Eventually, the actual engineering and design technology are moved.

I participated once in a strategic move of a product line to Asia that included a great deal of technology and processes that I would have considered trade secrets. You don't patent trade secrets because that would make the information public and easier to reverse engineer. The company had sent me with a team of engineers to the selected supplier in China for the purpose of helping their staff understand how all the technology worked.

An interesting thing happened after the second week of those sessions. We were working late into the night with all our engineers sequestered in a large conference room. I understood everyone was tired, but when I looked around the group, one of the most senior engineers had his head in his hands. I asked him, "What's up?" After a pause, he looked up and said, "Do we realize what we are giving these people?"

That hit me like a ton of bricks. We had been so busy trying to achieve our assigned task that I had never considered that aspect of what we were doing. We were revealing the intricate subtleties of our technology that took many years to develop. We were giving up our "know-how." It is troubling to realize how many other U.S. companies are doing the same thing.

Another example occurred when I was working in the manufacturing engineering area at a large automotive steering systems
supplier. My group was responsible for ordering all the machines
and equipment used in our production processes. The managing
director of that area learned of a similar factory that had recently
closed operations for a move to China. He asked me to tour the factory to see if we might want to buy any of their idle equipment.

This was an exceptionally large factory, so I scheduled an
entire day for the visit and took along several other engineers. A
special guide was waiting for us when we arrived. He had already
arranged for all the lights to be turned on throughout the multiple
buildings. As I began walking down the endless columns of huge
industrial machines, I began to feel really sad. No, that's not right. I
was feeling a little sick. At one point, I walked over to one of the big
machines and said to our guide: "Do you have any idea how long it
takes an operator to become proficient operating this machine? ...
Or, that one? Or that one? We ended the day buying some excellent
equipment at bargain-basement prices, but it was not an experience
I could feel good about.

I noted a recent statistic stating that in 1965 manufacturing
accounted for 53% of the economy. By 2004 it accounted for just 9%.
I know that when I was growing up, my dad worked in a factory.
All my friend's dads (and many moms) worked in factories. They
were good jobs, paying good wages, manufacturing goods that were
competitive worldwide. They were the jobs that fed the middle-class.
Now, with so many industries having abandoned their U.S. facilities,
there are very few jobs that provide a middle-class income. I suspect
that not having these middle-class jobs is one of the reasons that
welfare rolls have exploded. This also doesn't sound like a sustainable
condition for a healthy America.

Nevertheless, the tip for improving your career in a large company is to propose moving manufacturing out of the U.S. This can improve profits, and anything that improves your company's profits will benefit your personal status in the company.

However, that action should not be taken lightly. After all, your company is simply a bunch of people who know how to do something. When you give those people away, you're giving away part of the company.

* *   * *   * *

When I step back from the point that I am making of advancing your career by suggesting offshore sourcing, I can't help but speculate about ways to reverse the trend. How, for example, does Ireland achieve adequate funding without large taxes on companies? The answer is that they tax individuals at a much higher rate than in the U.S. (over 40%). Wages have to increase to compensate, but that might change the incentive to move profits, and jobs out of the U.S. Today, when costly new programs are proposed in the U.S., politicians are more inclined to increase taxes on companies because companies don't vote them in or out of office. The fact that this action helps to move jobs out of the U.S. is lost in the political fog. We will talk more about this in the Afterward.

1. FIND THE RIGHT FIT

Know Thyself

The opportunity for moving up in an organization is probably 30% credentials and experience, 30% luck, and 40% personal attributes.

You probably know what I mean regarding "personal attributes": "Old Joe" will never make manager, given his personal attitude and offensive disposition." It is simply personal characteristics that make Old Joe obnoxious, strange, or undesirable. Of course, sometimes those personal characteristics can be an asset to the organization. A hardheaded employee is often the absolute best person to drive schedules and ensure project completions.

An area I managed was once assigned to manufacture a new product, which included a critical component that seemed to be un-manufacturable by known processes. We assigned Old Joe the part and told him it could not be made. A year later, Old Joe had put together a process that involved using a unique procedure available only in England, a special machine made in Brazil, a special material available only in Japan, and a special treatment being developed for the space industry in California.

The project was a hands-down success. Anyone else would have given up. (I had.) Old Joe simply could not give up.

His stubbornness had actually saved the program. Should we promote Old Joe? Heavens no! He offends almost anyone he encounters. No one could tolerate working for Old Joe for long. The personality attributes, which make him so offensive, would be very difficult for him to change. But would we give him a bonus? You bet!

You may have ingrained attributes like Joe's obstinacy * and confrontational style. Unfortunately, those traits will prevent you from being on the management candidate list. But the good part is that you may become the most valuable (and well-paid) member of a team.

You may be saying, "I know I am difficult (or some other perceived negative attribute), but I can change." If that is your attitude, and you are sincere, you may be able to make changes. However, my experience predicts that you would be better off using that attribute as a strength and taking pride in being the one who makes things happen instead of trying to be the boss.

The point in knowing thyself is to try to understand who you are now and who you would like to be tomorrow. Figuring that out is a difficult task. Fundamental aptitude and personality tests (i.e., Myers-Briggs, etc.) can be helpful. But your time would be spent more wisely thinking about what you like to do, what you have been good at doing, and what the combination of the two means. Then you can figure out how to create a plan for earning the credentials and experience that will put you on a path for personal success. And if that plan has nothing to do with moving up in an organization, then you can stop reading now.

I used to get upset at old friends who had shown such talent and intellectual ability in their early years but chose professions that involved manual, semi-skilled labor. But then, as I got older, I realized that their life choices had not been a failure on their part. On the contrary, it had been a choice. They chose happiness over financial gain. They had lived lives that provided all of life's necessities, without the stress of the pressure jobs.

Many people shun an opportunity for management because of the fear of additional stress. Actually, stress is caused by being threatened or being in a situation over which you have no control. For example, assembly line work can be very stressful. Workers on the assembly line have almost no control over their job and are under constant pressure to keep up. Managers often have more control of their jobs and, therefore less stress than their employees. A good manager will remember that. It can help him be a sensitive and more effective manager by recognizing the potential stressful environments of employees.

This is not to imply that management cannot be an incredibly stressful choice. It certainly can. The stress, however, is often the result of the pressure the manager puts on himself for achieving success, along with the added time involved in that pursuit. The personal sacrifice of this added time dedicated to work also frequently results in a more stressful family life.

* *   * *   * *

I will be talking a great deal about credentials and how to position yourself to be a candidate for moving up the ladder because that component is the only factor under your complete control. However, I also talk about luck in some detail because there are things you can do to influence "luck," like being in the right company and being visible. And finally, as you see the kind of personal attributes you must have to achieve upward movement, you will have the option to consider modifying behaviors that could help you become a candidate for promotion.

Understand Management Candidate Requirements

You have determined you are not an "Old Joe" and therefore are capable of moving up the ladder. Here is a short list of characteristics that people on the candidate list usually have:

1. Have the right education (Life is like a camera...when things don't work out...take another shot.)

You rarely use very much of what you learned in school, on the job, but not having the proper college degree can be a fundamental barrier to being included on a management candidate list. It's unfortunate, but fact, nonetheless.

I developed a canned speech that I would give to newly hired engineers after they had been on the job for six months. At that point, they frequently came into my office saying that they were not using all the skills that they had learned in college. My reply was that we hired them because they had spent those college years learning how to solve problems by using the physical laws of science. What we needed was for them to solve our problems the same way.

That reply got them out of my office, but it also pointed out the fact that much of what is learned in college will be forever unused. However, having a degree is still a must for keeping your résumé on the desk with the other candidates.

Surprisingly, your grades do not seem to correlate with eventual career success. Nevertheless, grades are perceived to be the best criteria for hiring new employees by most large companies. For example, when I worked for IBM they were only interviewing candidates with a 3.5 GPA or above. This fact means that your options for a first job will be much better if you have maintained a good average. Maintaining a good average takes only a little extra effort. It takes a great deal of effort to pass a course in college. It only takes a little more to make a good grade.

It was Winston Churchill who made that famous speech about never giving up. It is especially good counsel relating to earning a college degree. So many times, I have seen students change majors or drop out because of one bad experience at college. As a result, they forever lose a chance at their dream careers. Start over at a different school, or simply repeat the try, but don't give up! You may think you don't have the brains or the skill, but you are wrong. All you lack is the will.

2. *Create a professional résumé and cover letter*

Your first introduction to a hiring manager is going to be your cover letter and résumé. That résumé has to pique his interest enough to call you in for an interview. Ideally, you ought to have several versions of your résumé contingent upon the demands of the job you're applying for. This is especially important if you have a long and varied background.

What you are doing at this point is selling what they are trying to buy. You stand a much better chance of catching their eye by emphasizing your background that meets their needs. This means you will need to thoroughly research each prospective company to anticipate their needs.

In my field, one company might need a strong project manager, while another is looking for someone with outsourcing experience, while still another needs a quality control person. If the job is in coding, it might be front-end, backend, cloud services, low-level algorithms, GUI design, etc. Every opportunity will have specific needs. Chances are, in your work experience, you have touched one of these areas during your previous jobs or schooling. Creating a résumé to emphasize your workplace experiences that meets that specific opportunity increases your chances of being placed into the stack of candidates under serious consideration.

The first rule in creating a professional résumé is to make sure it is **grammatically correct**. For example, if you are an engineer or other technical person, have someone above your experience level carefully proofread your résumé. I am not saying that engineers can't write proper English, but as an engineer myself, I am saying, "better you do I say what, than do not what I say do." (I told my English professor sister not to correct that sentence, even though I didn't see anything wrong with it.)

On a serious note, as I sought to fill positions in the companies I worked for, I have looked at hundreds of résumés over the years. It would always start with the personnel department bringing me a stack of résumés. As I tried to get quickly through the pile, if I ran into a grammatical error or two in the first few sentences, I slid that résumé into the trash can. So, don't be a slider. Put time and effort into this critical task.

Your word processor will undoubtedly have rudimentary checking. However, far better is using one of the cloud-based AI systems to critique your writing. I use Grammarly which has a free version, but the premium version is well worth the small investment. Watching it work will make you wonder where AI will take us in the not-too-distant future.

The second rule is to state **what you accomplished** as opposed to your job description. What I need to know as a hiring manager is what contribution you made to that job. Did you make an improvement? What was it? Did you learn something relevant? What was that? Too often, what I would see is simply company job descriptions for each listing. What I wanted to see is what you did, personally.

Having one or two sentences at the top of a résumé that summarizes experience and lists core competencies can be immensely beneficial. Frequently, companies use software to search résumés for keywords. When the software finds the right keyword, it can tag that résumé for further review. The stack of résumés I was receiving from H.R. often had keywords highlighted that I had identified in my hiring request. If you are responding to a job opening, you can often find a keyword or two in the posting. If they fit your experience, be certain to include them in your customized résumé.

A third rule for writing a résumé is **brevity**. One page is excellent. Two pages are OK, but any more and you've lost me. Your thick résumé has become another slider. This also means that keywords and accomplishments become even more important. By including your contributions, companies can see that you can hit the ground running.

The cover letter is where you highlight experience or a personal situation that sets you apart. For example, working your way through college can be a real plus, but not apparent on a résumé. Call attention to specific experience that might be applicable to the job opening. You can also include personal aspirations that might fit their opportunity.

Another "slider" for me was seeing a resume of someone who seemed to change companies every year or two. I suppose I was assuming that this person could not hold a job for long. The cover letter is where you could explain circumstances that might have led to those job changes. Of course, seeing an experienced person's resume who had advanced at the same company for many years tended to end up on the top of the stack. Just like the résumé, the cover letter must be brief and to the point. A couple of paragraphs should suffice.

Before you wallpaper the world with your resume you need to answer a few questions: Am I willing to relocate? If so, do I have a preferable geographical area? How can I get the greatest exposure in those areas? What kind of company do I want to work for? Do I know anyone at any of the prospective companies who might help? Which websites will best suit my search needs?

As you see in much of this book, relationships will always be important for professional success. With regard to having your résumé considered, often someone you know who is employed by that company can help. Once, a family friend told me that his son was applying for a job at the company where I worked. I offered to deliver his résumé to H.R. so that he would not have to mail it and endure a tedious chain of command.

I offered, because I knew this family and had known that the candidate was a good worker as he had helped his dad and me on several house improvement projects. That next week, I walked down to the H.R. director's office with the résumé. As I noticed him alone and doing some paperwork, I pecked on his door. He motioned me in, and when he finished writing a few lines, he looked up at me. I told him that I was simply delivering a résumé from a candidate I could vouch for.

He took the résumé but didn't look at it. Then he looked up at me and said, "He's hired." I said: "Wait a minute. I was just delivering this résumé. I didn't mean to have any influence on hiring. I don't have any influence on this opening." He said: "You don't understand. I interview this guy for 30 minutes; I know a little more. But you know a lot about this man, and I know a lot about you. He's hired. And besides, when he works here, he has two bosses instead of one. He has his direct manager, and he has you." I gulped, thanked him, and left his office. The point, of course, is to not be bashful about asking for help from someone who might walk your résumé to the right person in a company. It invariably helps.

Make a **follow-up phone call** to the company to check on the status of the application. A company I had been with for seven years asked me to move to corporate headquarters (in the frigid North). My daughter was very involved in her school at that time and my spouse certainly did not want to move. As I thought about the situation, I remembered that IBM was building a new site in our city and wondered if moving companies might be a solution. I sent a résumé and cover letter to IBM but received no reply, no interview invitation, no form letter rejection, nothing. After a few weeks, I decided to follow up with a phone call.

The phone call seemed to fall into the black hole of enormous company bureaucracy as I bounced from one person's voicemail to another. However, I didn't give up and kept occasionally calling during the next two weeks. It was becoming something of a game for me to see whose voicemail I would be transferred to next. Finally, I specifically asked to talk with the H.R. director. He answered the phone and, after I explained a toned-down version of my reason for calling, asked me to hold on for a minute.

A couple of minutes later, he told me that I was supposed to have been contacted about coming in for an interview. He then asked when I could come in. I told him that it would have to be Saturday because I was already in the frigid North. After another wait, he said that this Saturday would be fine. That Saturday, two midlevel managers were there to interview me and offered me a job on the spot. It was the best job move I ever made. But, more important, it was the best phone call I ever made.

Fifteen years later, I received a strange phone call about that H.R. Director. I had moved to a different site in the company, and the phone call was from an old acquaintance. He had just attended the retirement banquet for that H.R. Director. It seems that after all the roasting speeches were made, the H.R. Director went up to the podium to talk about his successful career with the company. The first thing he said was, "I hired Bob Vines." I assume that was his attempt to start his talk with a laugh, but it just reminded me of the simple phone call I once made.

Another example for follow-up phoning happened when the shoe was on the other foot for me. I was managing several engineering groups when I got a phone call from a friend of a friend. It seems that he needed to make a job move and was hoping to relocate in his home town, which was where our company was located. We were not hiring at the time, but I asked him to send a résumé, which I forwarded on to our human resources department. Then, once every month for a year, I received another follow-up phone call from this fellow. I may have ultimately hired him to stop the phone calls, but he worked out to be a very good engineering employee. Persistence paid off for him just as it had for me.

Finally, assume your resume could end up on your current boss's desk. That can be either a good thing or a bad thing, depending on your boss, and your standing in the current company. If you are a key contributor, it might trigger consideration for a raise. However, this could also be interpreted as a lack of loyalty and have a negative effect on your future, especially if you end up staying with that company. Either way, the possibility of your resume ending up on your boss's desk is a good reason **not to embellish or exaggerate** anything in your résumé, cover letter, or interview. (Unless you are running for political office.) Emphasize skills and experience that would be an asset to your candidacy for the job, but do not embellish or lie. Stretching the truth can put you in an uncomfortable job, or ruin your reputation.

Also, if you find that you need help with your résumé, do the same thing you always do when you need help: ask Google. There are many resources available for free. One that I have used is https://www.thebalancecareers.com/

3. *Look the part*

You need to look exactly like someone in the position you want to have. In the past, this meant spending a good deal of money on clothes. Today it means looking like the boss. If the boss wears expensive duds, then so must you. But most importantly, you must always look like a professional. For me, that meant taking my shirts to the laundry and getting a haircut every two weeks. I was hoping the extra cost was really an investment.

A young engineer came into my office once for an annual appraisal and personnel discussion. When he talked about his aspirations to become the president of the company, I decided to take a chance and be honest with him. (You will see later why being honest is taking a chance.) I told him that the first thing he needed to do was to get a haircut and spend $2,000 on clothes. People at that company who were on the candidate list were expected to look like executives.

The next day that engineer came into my office with heartfelt thanks for the advice and announced that he was going to become the best damn engineer that company had ever had. Fortunately for him, you could enjoy the same salary as an executive at this particular company if you were a very valuable individual contributor.

You have probably seen the data reporting that tall, thin people get more promotions. It is another fact in an unfair world. But for someone who wants to be on the candidate list, staying in shape is simply another item on the long checklist. Keeping off extra pounds can be a big part of being in shape.

Like many folks, I have a weight problem. Once, after realizing that I was 30 pounds overweight, I did some research and discovered a technique that has helped me maintain a steady weight. The first thing I learned is that we are all genetically predisposed to overeat. Food was difficult to obtain for our distant ancestors, which meant that those who overate when it was available were more likely to survive. This means that the overeaters were more likely to thrive and reproduce.

We are the inheritors of that perpetually self-refining selection process. This process pushed the trait of over-eating into our genetic makeup. One result today is that the sensory feedback signifying to the brain that we are sated is actually delayed by about 15 minutes on average. This phenomenon is one reason that slow eaters are less likely to overeat, and it is also the reason we often find ourselves feeling "stuffed" 30 minutes after a meal. We don't feel the effect until about 15 minutes after eating. That phenomenon has also been cited as one reason people in France, for example, and other cultures who cherish longer meals with multiple courses, tend to have less obesity.

I discovered that phenomenon while researching the subject to solve my own weight problem. I really liked one book on the subject, called "The West Point Fitness and Diet Book." It said: "Forget weight and height charts. Take all your clothes off and look in the mirror. That's the best way to tell if you need to change your lifestyle or eating habits." I didn't do that, but the mental picture of what I might see was an inspiration to make some changes in my life.

I especially appreciated learning about man evolving to over-eat. That meant that my problem was really not my fault. Evolution made me this way. What worked for me—to combat what evolution was doing to my body—was to try to **eat with my eyes** instead of waiting for my stomach to tell me "Enough." It is especially helpful to do this in restaurants where more food is always served than we should eat. I simply look at my plate as it is served and decide how much of it I should eat. Then, when I reach my target, I stop (or try to stop). I end up taking a lot of carry-outs home.

The second thing I learned is what kinds of food are good for me and how to **read labels**. I don't eat much red meat anymore or animal fats. I am lucky in this area because there is no food that I don't enjoy the taste of. I love the taste of a salad without dressing (which is often the bad stuff).

Of course, it is possible to move up in an organization looking different (like being way overweight or having a long beard or tattoos). But why create the barrier? Unconventional appearance is a barrier that some people will have to climb over to see the "real you." Many decision-makers will not bother climbing over that barrier. For the same reason, women who are interested in advancement should never wear revealing or flashy clothes. Looking different or unprofessional presents a negative stigma for some folks, and at least one of these people is probably in your upper management chain. The wise move is to simply not create that "first impression" barrier.

At one point in my career, I needed to move near my aging parents, which involved taking a much lesser position in a company in the region. I felt lucky to find a job with a, excellent company even though it represented a 30% cut in pay and moving from middle management to individual contributor. The only clothes I had to wear were the executive style suits which were customary in my previous job. One day, after about six months with the company, I noticed the top local executive talking with a higher-level manager in my chain as they walked in my direction. I could just barely hear him say to the executive: "Doesn't he even look like a future executive?" He was talking about me! Right then, I knew that I was "on the candidate list." And I knew that the "suits" were a part of the equation.

4. *Personal life = professional life*

Your personal life must be the same as your professional life. You simply cannot be a "professional" from 8 to 5. You have to be a professional 24/7. That means your social media cannot be filled with drunken weekend brawls and wild shenanigans.

One DWI can take a person off the candidate list. Early in my career, I made a big mistake by drinking too much on work nights. In fact, I had to change jobs to get out from under the reputation I had developed. In the process, I discovered that you could smell alcohol on my breath (actually acetaldehyde) the next morning after drinking in the evenings. So, the rule I developed was never to have more than two drinks per night (yes, a beer is a drink) and have nothing to drink after 7:00 p.m. on a work night. Fourteen hours is a good number to use for ensuring the effects are out of your system. And of course, never, ever drink too much at an office function. Don't even try to keep up with the boss. But don't make fun of him either. Simply be professional.

Socializing outside of work with other employees can build invaluable relationships, especially if they are in your management chain. If you are a new employee, determine the social culture in your company. Find out what "they" do in their free time and try to join in. It is probably going to be bowling or golf, but it could also be community volunteering. Find out what it is and join in. It might even be fun. It will surely give you the type of exposure that has enormous value when dealing with these same people at work. It always seems easier to ask for help at work if you already know the person from a social setting. For certain, you will be asking for a lot of help, especially early in your career.

However, never forget that at these company events, you are still at work. Therefore, your **behavior must be professional** at all times. One mistake in front of other employees can follow you back to the office and ruin your future. And, of course, watch what you say to others.

In my very first professional job, I related a story from my childhood that I had only partially witnessed. It seems that my dad was going to prepare a live turkey for Thanksgiving dinner. Apparently, he had done this many times because he took the time to show me the hatchet that had a blade cut flat to ensure a clean cut of the turkey's neck as he chopped off the head. He had rigged up a system where he tied a line to the turkey's foot and had strung it over the cloths line. He explained to me this was to keep the turkey from flying away after he cut it's head off. I was prevented from witnessing the actual "event" of this head removal by my mother who must have thought it too traumatic for my young eyes.

I happened to relate this story to a group of much older work companions in a social setting, many of whom had been raised on farms. They laughed and immediately started making fun of my "headless flying turkey." I figured out later that my dad probably was trying to simply keep the headless turkey from staining him with any blood if it flopped his direction. But at the time, I didn't know a headless turkey couldn't fly. It took years before my nickname of "Turkey Bob" went away. The point is: watch what you say. Listening instead, can be educational.

5. *Develop and protect your credit rating*

Not only do companies look at your social media in assessing candidates, but they also check your credit rating. A credit rating can be a good indicator of a dependable and responsible candidate.

My personal goal in my first real job was to save enough money to buy a decent used car. When I had finally saved up enough to buy the car, my boss recommended that I take out a loan for the vehicle instead. He said I needed to start establishing credit and also recommended getting a credit card.

I followed his recommendation, and it turned out to be good advice. I had a temporary work assignment many years later and decided to lease an apartment instead of staying in hotels. The renter's insurance policy I had chosen was to be mailed to the apartment. Instead, I received this strange phone call from the owner of the agency asking if I would mind if he delivered the policy personally. I asked why. He said he just wanted to meet someone with a perfect credit score. I later learned that I had been enjoying discounted rates on several things because of that score. But, of course, that was before I got married again.

6. *Sleep six to eight hours a night*

The brain doesn't function properly without adequate sleep. If you do become drowsy at work, you might need a sleep test. Sleep disorders can rob you of your brain. But, of course, the usual problem is simply staying up too late.

My problem with losing sleep was procrastination and time management. I have a little note pinned to my bulletin board: "Are you working on the most important thing?" I never read the message because important tasks are never as much fun as everything else. Putting off the important/less enjoyable activities causes me to lose sleep to catch up on necessary tasks. A good idea instead, is to review your to-do list often, and prioritize it. It helps if you designate on that list when you are going to do the top items. If something comes up during the day, add it to the list instead of interrupting your plans. Adding it to the list is smart, and it lets you go to bed earlier.

I have another note on that bulletin board: "**The Trouble is: You Think You Have Time**." Promising yourself that you will do something "tomorrow" brings great comfort and relief. The only problem is that tomorrow always has a way of becoming "now" with the same barriers that yesterday had. And the thing you had to do inevitability takes more time than you thought. That means that it is always better to embrace the "now" rather than the 'tomorrow." Do it now, and you can sleep tomorrow.

7. *Choose a compatible life partner*

If you are going to move up in an organization, your spouse needs to be someone who will tolerate your hours, your changing locations, and your moods. Not having that understanding and support can prevent you from achieving your goals and make both of your lives miserable.

As Gary Chapman says in his book, "The 5 Love Languages": "Drop the idea of finding a soul mate. We have this mythological idea that we will find a soul mate and have these euphoric feelings forever. In fact, soul mates tend to be crafted, not found. There are tens of **thousands** of people out there that anyone could be happily married to. And each marriage would be different." Each could be wonderful as well, but the key is that crafting that relationship takes **work**. You must constantly work to understand the other person, put your feet in their shoes, and recognize their needs.

Here are the top needs for women in marriage: 1. Affection, 2. Conversation, 3. Honesty, 4. Financial Support, 5. Family Commitments. The top needs for men in marriage are: 1. Sex, 2. Recreational Companionship, 3. Attractive Spouse, 4. Domestic Support, 5. Admiration and Respect. Look at that list. They are not even similar. Now, you can understand why the key to success in a relationship is work. That work is remembering the list and meeting the needs of the other person.

As you make this choice of a companion it is best then, to set emotions aside and spend some time analyzing attributes before making a commitment. Then, after the commitment, spend the rest of your life courting that person. If they tolerate and support you, you have found a treasure.

From an ethical standpoint, it is also better to stay away from romantic relationships with co-workers. That was hard for me because work was about the only environment where I had an opportunity for developing relationships (other than family reunions ... yes, I am from the South). I tried to resist relationships at work until I took an early retirement and then married my old H.R. manager. She had already learned to tolerate me. (No, it wasn't my first marriage or my second. But I can say that, although practice did make perfect for me, it is much better to do it right the first time.)

A final note on this subject: If you find yourself in an incompatible relationship, have the courage to move on. I failed to take that step at the right time in my life, which resulted in negative consequences for the child I thought I was protecting. While it is true that sometimes you can work out, and fix problems, sometimes you cannot. Be realistic about assessing the situation and then force yourself into a path for a tranquil life. Whether it involves fixing the problems, living single, or finding another partner, it will take dedicated and thoughtful effort on your part. Don't shy away from that task. The rewards can be a new life filled with happiness. As you seek that happiness, don't forget the key words: "**Thousands**" and "**Work**".

8. *Learn how to be interviewed*

You only have one chance to make a good first impression, and that impression can be the difference between receiving an offer and receiving a form letter.

The single most crucial aspect to remember before an interview is to **be prepared**. Know the company and how your skills might fit in. Practice answering all the likely questions you might be asked. Finally, create a list of questions of your own. Of course, the first step in preparation is finding potential questions on the internet along with all the standard tips on how to dress and act during the interview. As mentioned, the internet sites I like best for questions are Alison Doyle's "The Balance Careers" and "Career Tool Belt." They have excellent free guides covering the entire process for getting a good job.

When I was the manager interviewing folks, I must admit that 50% of my decisions were based on the résumé and how the person looked as they walked in the door. I will bet that is true for other decision-makers as well. So, what you look like that day is especially important. Always err on the side of being overdressed. You want to look like the job, but more importantly, you want to look professional. And you want to look like you want this job. If the decision-maker is like me, he is also trying to hire "attitude" along with skills. How you look reflects your attitude. (See section on "Hire a Bell Ringer." In Chapter 6)

9. *Have the courage to say no*
If you have found your passion, resist the ego pull to take a promotion or job change. Finding your passion turns work into a life of pleasure. Also, if you feel the offered promotion is in an area with a questionable future, have the courage to say no.

As a middle manager I once needed a technology manager and had decided on a manager who worked in another division of the company. I interviewed him and offered him a promotion. He surprised me when he turned down the job. In fact, I think that is the only time I have ever been flatly turned down when I offered someone a good job. It seems that he just didn't believe in our line of products. I was disappointed and mystified by his rejection.

As time passed, he did get promotions, eventually becoming a senior vice president of the company and my boss. He had the courage to say no when his vision of the long term was negative. (And his vision about my area had been right because a few years after I had offered him the promotion, the company closed down the business I was managing.)

10. *Never stop looking for another job*

When you are first hired, you are probably overpaid. However, as you learn the job and develop skills, your salary rarely keeps up with your abilities. Even promotions seldom result in significant increases in your pay. Unfortunately, the best way to earn a substantial increase is by changing companies.

Another reason to constantly be looking for another job is when opportunities seem to be rare in your company. This may indicate that your company is not growing. And if your current company is not growing, the chances of moving up are limited. Waiting for your boss to die or retire so that you can take his job can be a long, fruitless wait. (Especially with everyone feeling compelled to retire later in life these days).

I was promoted twice in my career with less than a year in my current job because company growth had created opportunities. Thinking back on those two promotions reminds me of a saying by Erasmus,

"In the land of the blind, the one-eyed man is king."

I am reminded of that because I was not a good choice for the new job, it was just that everyone else was a little worse. Growth had created the opportunity, and I was lucky enough to have ridden the ballooning wave.

Of course, finding a growth company these days is not always easy. Nevertheless, having growth potential as a criterion for choosing a company should be on your short list of considerations for employment. Also, if your current company is not growing, that fact should be a strong signal to be more aggressive in looking at other opportunities.

After a job change, you will always be the new guy in the department. Being that new guy can sometimes be an advantage. People who have been around for a long while are rarely promoted. I suppose everybody knows their faults and sees them as peers. If you are the new guy and have made a good impression, other workers are more inclined to accept your promotion. I'm not sure about all the reasons for that, but I have noticed it repeatedly. The wisdom is that if you have your eye on the job at the top of the company, you should always be looking to move along.

Another benefit from "moving along" is that you achieve valuable experience in multiple areas of a company if the move is internal. A move to a brand-new company can often allow you to experience an entirely new corporate culture. You will be amazed at how different corporate cultures can be at companies that seem to be in similar businesses. Having exposure to both cultures can make you especially valuable in your new setting. You will have opportunities to suggest changes for improvement that you know to have worked better in your previous company. Of course, you will need to be careful not to make the wrong impression by making suggestions sound like criticism or pushing for change too quickly. (You will read more on this subject in the section "When You Change Jobs, Do Nothing" in chapter 8)

I came to enjoy one aspect of looking for a new job particularly. During the job interview, the interviewers invariably give you a tour of their operations. They also seem to be much more open about innovations and the inner workings of their business than you would ever receive on a formal tour as a visitor. That benefit helped me decide to save one week of my vacation every year for interviews. Occasionally, I found myself returning to my current job with a brand-new idea of how to make things better based on what I had seen working well somewhere else.

Finally, here are some of the websites that I can recommend for locating a job.

Indeed.com

Indeed includes millions of job listings from thousands of websites, including company career pages, job boards, newspaper classifieds, associations, and blogs.

Job seekers may also search job trends and salaries, read and participate in discussion forums, research companies, and even find people working for companies of interest through their online social networks.

LinkUp.com

LinkUp is a job search engine that searches jobs on company sites. The job postings are from small, midsize, and large company career sections and are updated whenever the company website is updated.

SimplyHired.com

SimplyHired searches thousands of job boards, classifieds, and company sites. Advanced search options include the type of job, type of company, keyword, location, and the date the job was posted.

US.jobs

US.jobs lists thousands of jobs directly from company websites and from state job banks. The site is run by the National Labor Exchange, and is provided by both DirectEmployers and the National Association of State Workforce Agencies (NASWA).

Niche Job Search Engine Sites

Niche job search engines search for jobs based on specialized criteria like type of position, career field, industry, and jobs posted on sites like Twitter.

11. *Don't let pride interfere with your judgment*

I once went into my boss's office and told him that I needed a 100% increase in pay. After he stopped laughing, I told him that I had an outside offer of a 120% increase. I then said to him that this would be my two-week notice. Two weeks later, the local company executive called me into his office. I expected him to say goodbye and to wish me well. I was stunned when instead, he offered to match the outside offer. I wanted to tell him, "If I was worth that much, why haven't you been paying me that much?" I didn't say that, but it was my pride that kept me from accepting his offer. I had also made a commitment to the new company that I felt obligated to honor. I regretted that refusal of the matching offer for years because the new job, with the new company turned out to be a real disappointment. It is impossible to second-guess decisions like this, but the point is not to let pride push you toward a wrong choice or decision.

A good friend may have made that mistake when he graduated from college. The college had a career day, which included companies that set up booths in the gymnasium where new graduates could fill out applications. The company he had his heart set on working for was General Motors. That booth had the longest line for turning in applications. After a long wait to give his application to the G.M. representative behind the table, he was told he had to redo the application because he had made a trivial mistake. That person refused to allow him to simply correct the mistake. He filled out another application, waited another hour in line to turn it in, and then dropped it on the desk and left. He later got an invitation for an interview but turned it down. He let his pride over the discourteous treatment of one person prevent him from pursuing his dream of working for G.M.

The point here, it is easy to let your emotions cloud logical judgement. When you feel offended or angry, the best action is to **walk away**. Make decisions later after you have had time to put perspective on the facts and circumstances. Bouncing the situation over with a good friend can also be very helpful. Then, go kick butt.

2. DEVELOP SKILLS

Become a Good Salesman

Much of what you achieve in life will depend on how well you sell yourself and your ideas. Late in my career, I was moved in to manage a program that I later determined would have been a bad project for the company. When my management reluctantly agreed with me, I was left without a job. As a result, I was assigned to a job as a salesman, which was where the company did have openings. After two years in sales, I discovered that I had learned some valuable career lessons. I found myself wishing I had had that experience much earlier in my career.

As a salesman, I learned techniques for working with the kind of people that I usually tried to avoid. It allowed me to develop an understanding of the why of their views, as well as ways to meet their business needs. But most importantly, I learned that almost everything I had ever done involved sales. Whether I was trying to sell management on my ideas or sell my people on our company's plans, I was always selling. My success was totally dependent on how well I did that selling.

One sales lesson I learned is never to miss an opportunity to **learn professional techniques**. I had no idea how studied, and scientific the art of the sales profession had become. For example, there are interesting techniques that can be used for classifying a potential customer so that you can understand what might be most important to that particular personality type. Some folks value their time over anything else. Others need to establish a relationship before trusting a salesman. You will also find that these sales skills become valuable in areas other than the sales profession.

I had a boss once who was one of the rare executives who worked only eight hours per day. As a result, it became easy for me to conclude that his time was one of the most important things to him. As a result, I started more carefully preparing for meetings with him. I always tried to go to him with a set of crisp points (often on PowerPoint), with clear options and recommendations. I could then zip through a reasonably complicated topic efficiently and quickly. I believe he genuinely appreciated it. It may have been one reason he chose me to head one of his areas of business.

Contrasting with this manager and his personal-time priority, was another boss I had who loved to talk about the news topic of the day before beginning a business meeting. Then, the meetings always included long discussions covering, in great depth, the meeting's subject. Some of his meetings lasted far into the night before reaching the decision point. Relationships were obviously important to him. Recognizing that, helped me to deal with him, as well as tolerate the long meetings.

It was the sales training about understanding how to classify and satisfy the needs of different personality types that helped me be successful in working with both of these managers. The same techniques can help you with all your personal relationships. You will find it much easier to be a friend if you have an appreciation for what is likely most important to a particular person. You will also find that all successful sales seem to flow from successful relationships. Formal training can help you with techniques that enhance the building of these relationships. These techniques go far beyond the usual gifts and favors traditionally associated with salesmen.

One of the more effective sales techniques is often despised by professional purchasing managers and buyers. It is called backdoor sales. That technique is where the salesman bypasses the purchasing department to go directly to engineering or operations employees who have influence in purchasing choices.

When I joined IBM, one of their main products was mainframe computers. Almost all of those computers were leased from IBM rather than purchased. The lease came with on-site technicians from IBM to help operate and program the computers. These on-site technicians were perfect backdoor salesmen because they had daily access to customer employees.

Recognizing this added benefit of the backdoor sales, I was surprised when IBM announced that it was going to sell off all of those computers to each customer at a reduced price. This had the effect of significantly exaggerating IBM sales and profits for two years, but as customers tended to hire the technicians, IBM lost their best salesmen. (I was surprised, that is, until I realized that executive bonuses are based in large part on the annual sales and profit figures. More on shareholder capitalism later in the Afterward.)

Backdoor sales techniques apply to daily activities in large companies just as they do for product salesmen. For example, when you are trying to make a proposal to a decision-maker, it is always a good practice to sell his key staff first. They are the ones who can support you in a meeting or even help you with selling your proposal.

Another good sales skill is to learn how to **research your potential customer's business** so that you can emphasize your product features that might help meet its needs. It is also essential to design a presentation unique to each customer and be prepared to quickly adjust that presentation if there is less time allotted than you need. And, of course, it is essential to dress appropriately. This means dressing in a manner that presents you as a professional.

Just as I was surprised to discover how much information is available on the science of selling and the value of that learning in all professions, I recommend taking classes and checking into the many books on sales techniques. Especially helpful for me was the insight into determining what might be important to each customer and how your product or service could meet those needs.

Master Negotiation Techniques

As much of your job includes being a salesman, your success in that role will depend upon your negotiation skills. Understanding the techniques that have been developed to assist in this process is a real asset.

There is a plethora of consultants and courses available that help you develop negotiation skills. However, as you invest in that training, you will find that the most important considerations involve having adequate information for understanding the other party's wants, needs, and the environment in which you are operating.

An executive from one of the largest manufacturers of plastics raw material once visited the company where I worked to present a cost increase coming in the types of materials we were buying from them. He argued that oil prices were going up, which drove his company's costs up. After his presentation, I went to the whiteboard and outlined my understanding of his process. The main point I was making was that the primary building block of the plastics we were buying was ethane, which came from natural gas, not oil. Natural gas prices had actually dropped at that time. After another hour of discussing that process, we achieved a slight cost reduction instead of the intended cost increase. Having the correct information had enabled us to negotiate effectively.

The person with the most information is always the best qualified to negotiate. Unfortunately, most companies assign the negotiation responsibility to buyers who are frequently not familiar with the product or service being purchased. The better choice is the person who best understands the other company's products and business.

By **understanding the other party's needs,** you often discover factors such as timing and long-term commitments that outweigh the usual pricing issues. I once negotiated significant cost savings from a supplier by simply placing a purchase order immediately for raw materials that we would not need for several months. That company was getting close to the end of its physical year and desperately needed to improve its booked orders.

Accommodating the other party's needs within an acceptable framework of your position leads to final agreements and a successful negotiation. It is all about how to find the "win-win." And seeing that win-win will always be easier if you have the proper training in techniques as well as a solid understanding of the subject matter.

Perfect Presentation Skills

More often than you think, you will be asked to make a presentation in front of decision-makers. For many of those decision-makers, that presentation, that wink of time, is all they will ever see of you, and it can sometimes make, or break, your chances of career success.

Early in my career, I was honored by being elected to vice president of the regional American Management Association. At the first meeting where I was to introduce the speaker, I realized that every manager in my entire chain, along with more than 100 other managers, were in the audience.

I stood up. I walked to the podium—and passed out. I actually caught myself falling and stood back up, but I could not speak. My voice didn't work. I was simply so filled with stage fright that I could not talk. The organization's president stepped in making a joke that I had caught something in my throat and completed the introduction. That event remains high on my list of most embarrassing moments.

Another time, I was asked to make a presentation to a group of IBM executive board members at the last minute. I didn't lose my voice at that time, but I sure screwed up the presentation. I was relieved to learn later why I screwed up so severely standing on my feet. It seems that when you are under extreme stress, the fight or flight syndrome shuts down the thinking part of your brain. You really can't think. It helped me to understand that there was a reason I sometimes said stupid things in front of crowds.

The good part is that I learned I could overcome this. (And, if I can, anybody can.) I joined Toastmasters and began to study public speaking. After a couple of years, I found that I could give a decent presentation with few regrets afterward. I started to give talks at church as well as professional organizations. A pinnacle for me was when a stranger called me at home to ask where I would be speaking next. He wanted to bring friends to hear me. What a compliment! And I am fairly certain that my mother didn't put him up to it.

I learned many helpful strategies in Toastmasters, such as how to prepare and read the audience, but the most important lesson was to **practice**. After I knew how important it was, I occasionally noted that my actual presentation was the 50th time I had made the talk. Of course, the first 49 were made standing in my bedroom. I used my bedroom with the door closed because the practice I am talking about is not reading over your talk; it is actually saying the words.

While saying the words is absolutely essential, you also have to be careful not to lose the proper cadence and timing while speaking. I am sure you have witnessed a speaker racing through a presentation (often reading it) and lose the essential emphasis on the points of the talk. Proper timing is especially important in making a point. Jack Benny, the famous comedian, had this talent of turning his head and pausing before hitting his punch line that was magical. You can have that same magic in your talk if you simply slow down and focus on the points you are trying to make rather than the anxiety in your stomach.

Practicing also helps with the stage fright because having all the words you are going to say solidly in your memory allows you to deliver your talk regardless of your mindset or shaky hands. On the other hand, there are actions that you can take that simply address stage fright. The first thing is to focus on the message you are trying to deliver. You are there to say something to this audience that is important to you. Focus on getting that message across. Zig Ziglar, a legendary motivational speaker, says he did that by talking to only one person at a time. He would look at one person in the audience, speak a few sentences, and move on to another person to continue that one-on-one talk. Talking to one person at a time instead of an entire audience kept him from having to deal with all those focused eyes.

A final stage fright technique is to take a beta-blocker. There are a number of these, which all require a doctor's prescription. They work because they keep the heart from racing. A racing heart is the first of the symptoms that soon cascade into constricting blood vessels, which causes shaking hands, among other symptoms. They're all part of the fight-or-flight response called hyperarousal. Preventing that first symptom of a racing heart from starting appears to stop the panic associated with a temporary fear like being in front of a crowd. I tried this once, and it seemed to help, although I was never sure that I wasn't simply benefiting from the placebo effect. After all, if I thought I was not going to get nervous, I didn't get nervous. Now, I have to figure out how to trick my mind into thinking I have just taken a pill, when I haven't.

Understand Body Language and Nonverbal Clues

A host of body actions and facial expressions reveal how a person feels and what they are thinking. Understanding these non-verbal clues can give you a significant advantage in achieving favorable communication.

I had just finished a class on nonverbal communication the prior week when I took a small sales team to a major potential customer to present a proposal for our company to do an exceptionally large project. As I glanced around the conference room during introductions, I noticed something. The principal decision-maker in the room had assumed a classic negative posture. He had already made up his mind, and I was sure it didn't include our company.

As our salesman stood up to make our presentation, I stopped him. I then turned to the decision-maker and told him that we had this presentation showing how we could do their project and why it was a good solution, but instead of going through it all, I would rather hear from them what an ideal solution would be. His mood completely changed. He thought for a little while, leaned forward (a good sign), and started talking. When he finished, I asked our salesman to skip the first four charts and show everyone number five. We had almost nailed his wishes. The rest of the discussion was about how we could cover the two points that we had not included. We got that contract, and it may have been because I had taken the class on how to read body language.

Being observant enough to notice the nonverbal clues can also be helpful when you are listening or communicating with anyone. Sometimes what someone is saying is not really what they believe. Understanding simple body language and facial expressions can reveal honesty or a lack of sincerity. It can also let you know when you are not communicating correctly.

These nonverbal clues are easy to master. With practice, using this aid in communication becomes second nature. Of course, everyone already does much of this naturally. Formal training and refining those skills can make you even better.

Study the Differences in International Cultures

More and more companies today operate in the international arena. Understanding how cultural differences can influence business conduct abroad can be the difference between success and failure when working outside the USA.

The day after I arrived in Japan on one of my earliest visits there, I developed a terrible head cold. (The loss of sleep, long flights, and cramped airplanes seem to encourage head colds.) I was a member of a small team trying to establish a supplier for a twenty-million-dollar project. As this would be an exceptionally good contract for the potential supplier, we were naturally receiving a somewhat royal treatment. On the first day with the potential supplier, we were taken to a fancy geisha house for lunch. As I sat down on the floor cushion beside my assigned geisha server, my nose started running like crazy. I whipped out my handkerchief and blew my nose, as I normally do. As I was doing it, I noticed that my assigned Japanese guide across the table was looking at me a little strangely.

After struggling through the uncomfortable lunch, I took my Japanese guide aside and asked why he had had that look on his face. He politely told me that blowing my nose at the table in Japan would be similar, from an etiquette standpoint, to dropping your drawers and mooning someone in the U.S. Had I known, I would have excused myself and gone to the restroom. I had certainly gotten off on the wrong foot with the supplier.

I discovered another cultural mistake when we were hosting a group of Japanese business managers whose company was working with us on a new program. It seems that they would be staying through the weekend and requested help on where to play a round of golf. I am a terrible golfer and, rather than embarrass myself, asked one of the managers who reported to me, if he would take them to an excellent course near our plant. He was a scratch golfer and was delighted to be their host for the day while having the company pay for his round of golf.

When my "host for the day" returned to work Monday, he came into my office and reported that they had a great day except for one thing. He said that they kept moving their boss's ball or incorrectly adding up his score. What we didn't understand is that the boss is always supposed to have the best score. As this great golfer reported to me, I told him that he needed to take a lesson from that and adopt the same practice when we played together. That is what I told him, but I realized that I should have been the one playing that round of golf. There would be no need to cheat with me playing.

I made many similar mistakes during my early business trips abroad. However, the more important ones had to do with customary expectations in doing business. Asia is where you will find the most significant differences from customary practices in the United States. How you negotiate, when you have some of the most important discussions (very late at night, after many drinks), and how you run a factory can all be drastically different from what you have been exposed to in the U.S. For example, in China, the best way to operate a factory is through a Chinese-owned partner company. (My company lost millions learning that lesson.) Partners can navigate (side-step) the complex government regulations in a way not possible for outsiders.

It was easy for me to be attracted to Asian culture, particularly when visiting Japan. My attraction to Japanese culture began with my first visit. The plane landed in Tokyo late in the evening, and I had to take a taxi to the hotel. Before I could sit down in the back seat, the driver changed the little white doily on the back of the seat and held the door open for me. That seemed a bit unusual to me. Then, as we drove toward the hotel, I noticed that the driver turned the headlights off at the intersections. I soon noticed that all the cars were turning their lights off at intersections. I assumed they were trying to save energy, but as an engineer, I guessed the actual effect would be to wear out the light switch.

Then, I noticed that lots of folks on the streets were wearing dust masks on their faces. (This was long before the covid actions.) I had not seen that much air pollution but assumed that was the motivation. It was not until the next day that I came to realize that these things were all tied to the Japanese culture of respect for other people. The lights were being turned off to keep from shining in the eyes of the opposing cars. The dust masks were there to keep others from becoming exposed to the cold that the masked person may have had. If you show similar respect for others in your business dealings in Japan, your business will be welcomed.

I noticed another example of cultural respect the next day as I went shopping for electronics in Akihabara, the section of the city dominated by everything electrical. There were hundreds of tiny stores that all seemed to have the special of the day in huge piles sitting out front on the sidewalk. The amazing thing about this to me was that at night, they simply covered them up with a tarp and went home. Although any passerby could have reached under the tarp and stolen some of the products, that simply didn't happen in Japan.

At that time, my company was trying to market credit card teller machines in Japan and found that they were the wrong product there. The Japanese simply could not understand why our machines were encased in a vault made of one-inch-thick steel.

On the day of our flight home, we had no meetings and decided to tour an ancient castle in Matsumoto. From there we would go on to the airport. Our Japanese host hailed a taxi for us and volunteered to show us the castle. When we arrived at this impressive structure and left the taxi, our host said something in Japanese to the taxi driver. I then watched as the taxi drove off with all my worldly possessions in its trunk. My mind kept telling me I wasn't in New York City, but I was still very anxious about ever seeing my luggage again. Three hours later, as we walked out of the tour, there sat the taxi. (yes, the luggage was in the trunk)

Another example of this respect for others can be seen in the recognition of job status in the first introduction to a new person.

Introductions usually involve a ritual of presenting business cards to each person individually along with an appropriate greeting. The business card is always presented to the other person by holding it with both hands as you make a slight bow to the person you are meeting. Additionally, addressing someone is always by their last name followed by "San." I once asked a Japanese native if there was a point where two people addressed each other by their first name. He thought for a minute and replied, "If you had seen each other nude."

My company once had a chance to build a perfect alliance with a large Japanese company. As the prospects of a mutually beneficial alliance became more positive, we arranged a meeting to introduce the two companies' top executives.

The meeting was with our company's president in his private conference room. The president came into the conference room a little late, took one look at the people in the room, and said, "Oh, Japanese," and stepped back into his office. He came back into the conference room with a handful of business cards and threw them out on the conference table. As soon as he had thrown them out, he started talking about a couple of issues to be discussed about the agreements. His actions had just insulted the president of the other company, which probably contributed to our loss of that alliance.

As you become acquainted with cultural differences, you realize how they can influence your business's success globally. Just like the examples with Japanese companies, there are differences in every culture. The best way to accommodate and adapt to these differences is through training available from paid consultants and taking international culture courses. It is much better to have this training before you travel internationally. Of course, it is even better if you can learn a little of the country's language. You will always need to be able to say *Excuse me, Thank you,* and *I apologize.* And, if you spend time in

Italy, you need to be able to say *This is delicious (E delizioso)*, because it always is.

I learned a tip for getting along with my wife's Mexican family that might be useful if you are involved in work in Mexico. My wife said that I needed to know only two Spanish words: *Claro!* (*Right*), and *De veras!* (*Really*). She said that every time her Mexican relatives were talking in a group and looked at me, say one of those two words. I found it worked great. Of course, I also learned that the most important Spanish words for me were *Dos cervezas, por favor* (*Two beers, please*).

Of course, there are negatives associated with other cultures, like extreme ethnic and sexual discrimination that you often see. In the U.S., we also take ethical business practices of respect for intellectual property and fair treatment of labor for granted. We do not tolerate predatory pricing, bribery, or cybercrimes of any type. These values are not common internationally, particularly in Asian countries.

Often it was discovering the many negatives in other cultures that made me most appreciate my home country. I have a long list of things I would like to improve in the USA, but I have never, ever, been to a country I would prefer to live in.

That sentiment is shared by others. Early in my career, my company was a heavy recruiter of engineers in England. We were having problems finding the kind of experienced engineers who seemed abundant in the U.K. At that time, there were discussions of the "great brain drain," which I suppose we were a part of. The thing I noticed was how easy it was to persuade an engineer to make the move. Life was better in America.

Learn How to Conduct Business in Foreign Countries

My first association with China involved an attempt to set up our own factory inside China. That attempt failed because we simply did not understand the business culture and processes practiced in China. I remember one conflict arising after we had started staffing our assembly lines. We had been assigned a government overseer who I assumed was similar to a union steward in the U.S. When we notified him that we would be using 18 workers per assembly line, he thought for a minute and then said we would be assigned 55 workers for each line. Our people did not know how to deal with that. We simply did not understand how to get beyond this impasse.

Eventually, we learned that we had to hire a Chinese company to build our product in China. I am not certain how Chinese companies deal with that type of intervention, but it took learning that lesson to be successful in China. That lesson for operating in other countries seems to be a universal success factor. Hiring experienced local management and partnering with existing companies is always the best path for a U.S. company. Many companies specialize in securing the best foreign sources for your products. Using them can help keep you from making a poor partner.

Most other countries also have a much friendlier attitude toward industry than we see in the U.S. Generally speaking, all U.S. companies are understanding and sympathetic to environmental, health, safety, and labor regulations. However, the compliance bureaucracy in the U.S. can impose delays that stifle plans for expansion and growth. Other countries seem to streamline that process so much more effectively, which encourages growth.

I once tested the possibility of locating a highly automated factory in El Paso, Texas, rather than having it contiguous with our operations a few miles away in Juarez, Mexico. I ended up giving up on getting anyone in the U.S. to say if that would be feasible. Without complete environmental impact studies and regulatory approvals, no one would commit to the feasibility. However, there was no delay in achieving the required approvals in Mexico, and that's where we built the factory.

Travel Without Stress

Tips from a frequent flyer

Although I have flown a gazillion miles in the past 30 years, my very first flight is still one of the most memorable. I was about to graduate from college, and a company had invited me to their plant in Atlanta for an interview. The flight was uneventful until the landing. We must have hit an air pocket just as we were about to touch down because the plane slammed down on the runway and then bounced up again before settling down for landing. All the passengers yelled out while raising their hands in the air.

In my 30 years of flying, I have never had another landing like that. But, of course, it was my first flight, so I didn't think anything of it at the time. After all, we had made it just fine. The interesting part came on the flight home. You may have already guessed what I did. This time I had a window seat and could see when we were just about to land. And, sure enough, just as the wheels touched the runway, I raised both arms and screamed.

That was one of the first lessons on how to survive air travel. Following is a list of other tips that might help. Like my first lesson, they have been learned the hard way.

1.   Every time you park your car at the airport, park in the same row. You wouldn't believe how often I have wandered around a parking lot trying not to look like I was looking for my car. I found that I could look for my car without turning my head while walking with purpose and pulling my luggage. Also, park facing out. That makes it easier to get to your dead battery.

2.   Wear a sport coat or jacket on the airplane, regardless of the weather. Airplanes are usually too cold, and you can always use the extra pockets for tickets, passports, etc. The ladies will want a large purse that can accommodate snacks as well as the usual.

3.   Don't check luggage unless you have to. You don't need to take nearly as much stuff as you think. Also, you won't have to worry about retrieving luggage if you have to change flights because something gets delayed or canceled. When you've got your stuff with you, you can go with the flow.

4.   If you do check luggage, carry a briefcase or backpack. Here are some of the survival things to throw in it along with your paperwork: Earplugs (planes are too noisy)—I like the skin-colored foam ones, but noise-canceling earphones are much better. Extra pair of glasses if you wear them. Eye mask—the kind they give you in first-class to sleep. Blow-up headrest—keeps your neck from getting a crick when you sleep. Imodium A.D. and a mild laxative—trust me; if you travel a lot, you will thank me.

5.   As you get on board, start looking for where you are going to put your overhead stuff. Never put it behind where you are sitting. You will have to wait on everyone else to get off before you can get to it.

6.   Don't drink a lot of fluids on an airplane. I don't care what they tell you; it is too hard to get to the bathroom.

7.   If your personal plans and convictions allow it, consider having a glass of wine or beer. Some alcohol calms things down a bit on bumpy flights. (Note: "Some" means one drink.)

8.   Never put anything personal in the seat pocket. That is where you will leave it when you are rushing to get off the plane.

9.   If you hear an announcement that your flight's boarding will be delayed by 20 minutes (for any reason), start looking for an alternate flight. Twenty minutes of airline time usually measures about three hours on your watch. If you have to layover for the next flight, find a hotel with a shuttle service and enjoy the night. Don't take an early alternate flight unless necessary.

10.   Never pass a restroom without thinking about it.

11.   Thank the airline folks once and a while. They do an incredible job managing circumstances that are out of their control. (This will also get you much better results than criticism.)

Of course, there are lots of other travel options besides flying that you will be mastering. For instance, all big cities have mass transit options. This is sometimes the only logical option in Europe and Asia. I developed a love/hate relationship with "bullet trains". I enjoyed getting to the destination quickly, but I missed being able to enjoy the scenery along the way. So, be sure to check the internet before your trip to be familiar with the options. Also, do not be shy about asking for help. The courtesy of strangers will surprise you. I cannot count the number of times a stranger has walked me through directions. One fellow road the train all the way across Paris with me because he had concluded that I would never make it on my own.

3. DO YOUR JOB WELL

Understand your Company's Business (not just your job)

Read your company's 10K and annual report. Know the broad picture, as well as how your job fits into the business. Some day you just might have the opportunity to use the knowledge in a discussion with someone who makes decisions about people like you. It can give you an edge. Also, learn about the competition, as well as how your company differentiates itself from them. Another benefit of knowing your company's strengths is that it could help guide you toward the more strategic and visible jobs.

Shortly after joining a new company, I went by a McDonald's one morning to pick up something for breakfast that I could take into the office. As I stood in line, I noticed the company president sitting in a booth eating by himself. He had flown in from New York the night before to have meetings that morning. Instead of heading directly for the door after getting my food, I walked by the booth where the president was eating and simply made a comment about eating at McDonald's. He invited me to join him.

After taking a sip of coffee, I asked him about something I had read in the 10K report just a couple of nights before. He immediately started telling me "The rest of the story" and became so excited about the subject that he told me to come by his office so that he could show me a chart on the subject. After he excused himself to leave for the office, I dumped the rest of my McMuffin in the sack and rushed on to work.

When I arrived at his office, his secretary was already making me a copy of the chart he wanted to share. As I was taking the chart, the president came out of his office and asked my name.

A few months later, I attended a meeting where the president gave a talk to employees. I happened to have found a seat on the front row for the meeting. After a brief introduction, the president walked to the podium, pulled out his notes, looked at the audience, and said: "Hi, Bob." I guess I caught his eye, and he remembered my name. I spent the rest of the meeting trying to dream up a better story of why he knew my name because many people were going to ask.

Develop a Passion for Your Job

The two most important days in your life are the day you are born, and the day you find out why. That "why" can be your personal stamp on a profession. When you get passionate about your job, beautiful things can happen.

A senior vice president of a *Fortune* 500 company once related a meaningful lesson from his life. As a program manager, he oversaw a project that went terribly wrong, costing the company millions. As the department head, he had shouldered the responsibility because extenuating circumstances had a way of being ignored. As a result, he was taken out of mainstream management and assigned the position of quality manager, a dead-end job in that company. It was a penalty-box job that you usually never escaped from.

Instead of bitterly sitting out the usually tedious job of quality manager, the future vice president did something unexpected. He embraced the new job. It became his passion as he rewrote the entire inch-thick quality manual for the company. This new, innovative manual was so impressive that other companies began to copy it.

Marketing used it successfully as a tool to differentiate our company from the competitors. The quality manager received so much positive publicity that he was promoted, heading an entire division of the company. He had turned a dead-end job into a steppingstone.

If you think there is nothing in your job to be passionate about, you are wrong. There is always a way to make improvements and making improvements will get you recognition. When I graduated from college, I had my mind set on designing and building cars. I had worked for a few years for an automotive company while putting myself through school. And, I had always loved overhauling engines and working on cars. The problem, however, with my plan was that when I graduated, the automotive industry was in a slump and laying off rather than hiring new engineers. So, I ended up taking a job in a company that was in the electrical business.

That company needed help in their manufacturing engineering area that did the design of tooling and assigned me to that department. My first boss in that company said something unusual to me on the first day. He said: "You look pretty smart. Walk around and look for something that needs doing and do it." It seemed that he was a brand-new boss and very unsure of exactly how to organize and delegate.

My desk was in a veritable sea of desks and drawing boards in one large open area. The engineer whose desk was adjacent to mine had been hired to design the steel molds used in giant injection molding machines for making plastic parts. He had been building those for most of his career as a toolmaker and knew how they should be designed but admitted that he had a problem because he had never actually done technical drawing.

I immediately realized that I had found a temporary job with something that "needed to be done" because I spent three years as a draftsman and designer while working my way through school. My new job partner would talk me through what he wanted, and I turned those ideas into technical drawings. As a result, I began to learn a lot about plastics. I found the subject remarkably interesting, with the added benefit of providing excellent career potential because of the enormous growth in the plastics field at that time.

One year later, I was managing that plastics group, and seven years later, I accepted a job with another company to help manage their plastics division. I had become an expert. Plastics had become my passion. (Who needs cars when you can be passionate about styrene modified polyphenylene oxide?) Of course, as I moved into various management jobs, management became my passion. I even found that, as a manager, I could receive genuine vicarious pleasure in other people's accomplishments. That feeling was my reward for work that grew out of my passion.

Work Long Hours

Successful managers work extra hours. You may have known some who leave at five, but most work lots of extra hours. You make a favorable impression if you are on the job before the boss arrives and still there when he leaves. Everyone wants dedicated employees and putting in extra time is one of the best ways to show it.

After working for IBM for one week, my office mate surprised me with a comment he made to me early one Monday morning. He said, "We missed you on Saturday." Apparently, their culture included working more than 40 hours per week. Not following this practice would have harmed my chances of succeeding at the company. At other companies where I had worked, employees would have expected comp time for working Saturday. At IBM, extra effort was expected.

I was also surprised by the lack of employee complaints about the extra hours until I learned that the extra effort was a two-way street. The company's full-employment policy and unique benefits more than made up for the extra effort on employees' part. The atmosphere resulted in an unusually secure and effective work environment. I came to believe that it gave the IBM of that era a decidedly competitive edge.

Surveys consistently show that top managers average working fifty or sixty hours per week. I am not saying working extra hours is a requirement for success. But I am saying that most successful managers put in extra time. And, I am saying that putting in extra time makes a good impression on decision-makers. It is an easy way to demonstrate your commitment, and it can sometimes give you an edge over your peers as a promotion candidate.

Stay Squeaky Clean Ethically.

Occasionally, a supplier or salesman will offer you something tangible, or try to do a favor for you. It is tempting to accept. Sometimes it may be a small thing, like football tickets or a special golf club. Don't ever take it! Politely refuse under the guise of company policy.

A senior vice president and my boss called me to his office one day and started telling me a difficult decision he had to make that would mean a change in his life and his financial resources. One option allowed him to take advantage of a little-known company policy that would give him more money. When he finished telling me about the facts of the situation, I started pointing out the plusses and minuses of the different options. Finally, after talking for a little while, he interrupted me and said: "I didn't ask you to tell me about the trade-offs. I only ask you one thing: What would you do? I want to know what Bob Vines would do."

I had managed the purchasing department several years earlier and must have left him with an impression of insuring everything was strictly by the book. There were always temptations for buyers when salesmen would offer gifts as a way to influence or gain a good relationship with a buyer. Our policy was that you could not accept gifts. I defined a gift as anything worth more than $5. Anything less was a novelty and could be accepted, especially if it had the supplier's name on it—invitations to football games, etc. I classified them as gifts. I had one rule to go by: "**If you had to think about it, you couldn't do it.**" Apparently, my boss had wanted to do the right thing and thought that I would do that naturally. That was a genuine compliment. I suppose I shouldn't have told him that I would take the money and run.

I have seen excellent employees ruin their careers by accepting a gift or a special trip with the salesman and his wife. News always gets back to company management. When faced with that situation, always remember to "**think about it.**"--and, if you have to think about it...

However, there are cultural exceptions. For example, not accepting a gift in Japan or China can be a big insult. Of course, your appropriate plan is to be prepared to reciprocate if possible because that, too, is customary.

It is especially crucial to know your company's policy about any issue involving business ethics, like the example cited about gifts. Government law and regulations dictate many standards for ethical practice. However, many companies have extensive environmental, corporate social responsibility policies etc., which usually revolve around maintaining a stellar reputation. Becoming familiar with these is essential for interacting with others as well as for making everyday business decisions.

Never Ever Be Late

When you are late, you are sending a message. Unfortunately, that message is "I am more important than you," which is very disrespectful.

Several times I have heard a manager say, "We gave him the promotion because I can always count on him. He may not be the smartest, but he is always there." Being dependable is another way of treating everyone with respect. As Woody Allen once said, "**eighty percent of life is showing up.**"

While working in Mexico, I learned that I often had to walk from office to office and round up the staff for a meeting. I wouldn't say I liked it, but as a foreigner, I felt it was not a big enough issue to risk alienating the staff over. When a new corporate vice president took over the operation, he dealt with the problem much differently. His German heritage may have been the influence of his lack of tolerance for the cultural propensity not to be punctual.

Shortly after he took over the position, he had scheduled the human resources director to start the first three meetings by giving an update on a significant change in personnel policy. Unfortunately, at the first meeting, the HR director was late. By the time he arrived and set up, we had waited 15 minutes. In the second staff meeting the following week, the same thing happened. Then, when it happened the same way during the third meeting, I thought I could actually see steam coming out of the ears of that vice president.

In the fourth staff meeting, he calmly walked over, closed, and locked the door to the conference room at the appointed hour. It didn't take many staff meetings for the culture to change. That culture change soon began to trickle down through the ranks and improved discipline and efficiency throughout the organization.

Of course, to always be on time, you'll have to be early 90% of the time. That's not bad. You would be surprised how many opportunities develop before the meeting starts. Those early minutes are also a few moments when more casual conversations can help you build those important relationships you will depend on to accomplish tasks and achieve goals.

A final note on punctuality: If you believe it is OK to be late because you really are the most important person in the meeting, you are wrong. You are just a jerk.

Do What You Say and Only Say What You Know

Never make a commitment that you cannot complete. Never guess when answering a question. If you fall behind, don't go home until you catch up. If circumstances develop such that you know a commitment cannot be met, don't let your boss hear it from someone else. Instead, tell your story yourself, but first, have a recovery plan laid out. Integrity will be remembered.

The most valuable employees I ever had were folks who had become "delete keys" to me. When I received an email that required analysis and action by my group, I would typically forward the email to one of my staff with my comments and a request for them to handle the issue. When I forwarded these emails, I would usually place them in a follow-up file to make sure I checked back with the person later to be sure we had closed the issue.

That was my normal process except with a few of the best employees. When I forwarded the email, I didn't put it in a follow-up folder with these special employees. Instead, I simply hit the delete key on my PC. I knew from experience that this person required no follow-up. I could also count on feedback from them if there was a problem. Employees who become delete keys tend to move up in an organization.

Some of the most intelligent people I have ever known seemed to be able to answer any question on any subject. I never understood how they could remember so much information. The only problem with their answers was, that while 90% were correct, 10% were speculation based on what they thought the answer might be. They seemed to feel compelled to have a solution for everything. Some of the 10% might be correct, but some of it was absolutely wrong. I learned that I always had to check on their statements to make sure I had the facts.

By contrast, one manager, who reported to me, used to frustrate me by rarely being definite in answering a question. So many times, when I would ask him a question, he would reply, "Well, it could be this, and it could be that." Then he would talk about the "this and that" for a while, leaving me information but no answer. The great part, though, was if he answered, "It is this … or I will handle that," I immediately knew that I could take that answer to the bank. He never, ever, speculated or guessed. If he had an answer, it was right. Knowing that kept me asking his opinion.

Do Well What You Do

If a task has begun
Never leave it until it's done
Be the task great or small
Do it well or not at all

That little poem is excellent advice for anyone with aspirations of management. A friend had a plaque on his wall that said, "Do a Little More Than They Expect Every Day, and Every Day They Will Expect You to Do a Little More." In some ways, that is true. For certain, your boss will always appreciate your doing additional work. However, you will earn more recognition by doing one job well than doing many mediocre jobs.

I once managed a technology group. One of the great guys in the group had one peculiarity: He was very selective about taking on assignments. He didn't exactly refuse assignments, but he would often say that he was too tied up to help with a particular item. The reason he could get away with that subtle refusal of a task was that he did excellent work. When he did take on a job, the result always looked like a master's thesis. He invariably would receive enormous recognition for the work he did. In fact, he ended his career as one of the highest-paid technical folks in the company.

Remember the "quality manager"? Doing one job well, restored his status in the company and gave new vigor to his career.

Take the Initiative

Have you ever dealt with the government bureaucracy to get something done? If you have, you know that no government person ever takes the initiative. Any change or unusual request will require such delays that you sometimes simply give up. I finally gave up recently trying to change something at my house that required a permit. The clerk where I first applied, was about to approve it when he said, "I think I need to have this approved by my supervisor." After setting up a meeting with the supervisor, I was told that this had to be approved by the director. At my meeting with the "director", I was told that it had to first be approved by the water board, and then put on the agenda for approval by the city council. My permit was a small change that would have affected no one but me. I gave up.

The reluctance to take the initiative of all these people was undoubtedly because of fear of doing something slightly outside of the rules, regardless of how trivial it might be. In corporations, this can also become a factor in getting things done. Nevertheless, it is the risk taker who takes ownership of the issue that gets rewarded. Taking the initiative to fix or improve something will get you noticed. And those who get noticed often become managers. When in doubt, assume you have the authority – **ask forgiveness rather than permission.**

Practice "Completed Staff Work" Principals

The techniques that represent a guide for staff work should apply to every assignment. The concept includes a small list of rules to ensure that when you complete an assignment and present it to your manager, there is no need for follow-up or questions, only approval or rejection of your recommendation. Here is a summary of those simple, but important steps.

My understanding or definition of the problem, task, or opportunity is...

In many cases this is simply a restate of the assignment. However, it is essential to start with this statement, especially if you might be presenting to more than one person. This might also need to include why the problem exists and other related information.

The Data is...

This is where you gather and document the information needed to solve the problem. Spend adequate time on collecting and organizing this data because you must be able to analyze all the alternatives.

My analysis or evaluation is...

Sometimes this can be a simple list of pros and cons. It can also be separating the facts from opinions. Or it can even use statistical modeling or other research methods.

The options or alternatives are...

This is where you will be showing logical alternative solutions and would probably include cost, schedule, and results as well as risks. In some cases, it might include impact to other people, or programs. Think SWOT Analysis (Strengths, Weaknesses, Opportunities, Threats). Be sure to cover any barriers to the solutions.

My best recommendation is...

Point out the plan that has the greatest impact on solving the problem and best fits the objective and capabilities.

The data to support this recommendation is...

Explain why you have reached this conclusion. Present the data that supports this solution.

The plan for execution is....

You may or may not be the one executing this solution, but you should include a logical plan for execution.

The plan for tracking this solution is....

This is an explanation of how you would ensure this solution would be implemented, following the schedule and plan.

Following these simple steps help remind you how you should approach every job. They show that you are a professional. Remember my "delete key"? When an employee makes a presentation to me and I have no questions, I tend to add him to my "delete" key list. I also add them to the management potential list.

4. PREPARING TO MOVE UP

Be Visible.

The chance of getting picked for promotion is 30% luck. However, you can influence that luck by being visible.

When a young accountant at my company was selected to replace the accounting manager who had recently resigned, I was curious about the selection and stopped by the senior manager's office for a talk. I casually asked how the senior manager had made the choice. He said that he was sitting at his desk on the phone when he learned that an accounting manager was leaving the company for another opportunity. He said he hung up the phone and started thinking about who could take his job when he saw that accountant walk by. It occurred to him; this fellow could solve his problem. After all, he was an accountant and looked like an executive. I later learned that this account had made a practice of walking by the senior manager's office a couple of times each day. It may not have been the only reason that accountant was selected, but it sounded like it helped.

Even if this actual situation sounds too impractical to be something you would want to try, it still makes a point. Being seen by the decision-makers is an excellent way to influence your "luck." Becoming acquainted with decision-makers can be even better. Of course, you have to be careful. You want the decision-makers to know your strengths, not your weaknesses. Let friends get to know your weaknesses.

Volunteering for a task force or extra job can be an excellent way to be visible. It will give you exposure to other areas of the business and another set of managers while providing opportunities to establish new relationships. The best job I ever had started with a task force that I volunteered to participate in. The task force's mission was to envision a product and a process that would allow our company to get new products into the market quicker and at an affordable price point. That task force ultimately became an entire business area for the company, and I was lucky enough to play a key role.

Present a Positive Attitude

I am not saying that you have to be optimistic about everything (although it helps); I am saying to try always to **act positive**.

During one of our busier times, my company needed to choose a manager to oversee an exceedingly difficult program. I was certain that that new program's schedules and technical requirements would be next to impossible to achieve. As one of the interviewing managers, I was especially impressed by one particular candidate. He had obviously done his homework, as he brought with him to my session a list of problems and hurdles that would be particularly challenging to overcome. He had laid out an approach for the solutions but admitted that he could not guarantee success.

Another candidate came in with a totally different approach. He simply said that he had waited his whole life for this kind of challenge and was sure he could achieve complete success. I am not sure he even understood the requirements, but he indeed made a positive impression.

My boss was the real decision-maker on that selection, and he fell for the "success" man—hook, line, and sinker. The capable candidate, who probably had the best chance of managing the program, lost to the "always positive" "yes man" approach. No, he was not ultimately successful in meeting the program goals, but he did end up some years later as a senior vice president of the company. That single trait of always being positive continued to propel his career and represents a good tip for anyone interested in moving up in an organization.

As this positive attitude becomes second nature, you will notice that **when you change the way you look at things around you, the things around you tend to change.** (You will read more on this subject in the section on expecting employees to be what you want them to be, in chapter 6) And if you are like me and tend to be more of a "rise and whine" kind of person, remember; it is **often the squeaky wheel that gets replaced.**

Treat Everyone with Respect (everybody votes)

"He who lives to benefit only himself confers on the world a benefit when he dies." (Tertullian)

It is surprising how often a decision-maker selects an individual for promotion based on what he has heard from others about that candidate. What he heard, undoubtedly came from one of the candidate's peers or even someone outside of his organization. Keep this in mind in your dealings with everyone in the organization.

After receiving an unexpected promotion early in my career, I learned that one of the reasons for my being chosen for the position was a recommendation from an "Old Joe" guy who had been in the department forever. No one seemed to work well with Joe, as he was so insulting and negative about everything. I didn't like him either, but I had made a real effort to understand his ideas and had refused to simply argue with him the way everyone else did. Little did I know that he had the ear of our top executive. Apparently, he had recommended me.

My brother is a senior partner in a major law firm. One day he was having an important meeting with a few high-profile clients and, before starting the meeting, asked if anyone would like coffee. They all thought that would be nice. So, my brother buzzed his legal assistant in the next office and asked her to come in. Now I have to mention that a legal assistant is just as professional as a lawyer.

This particular assistant was excellent and an invaluable asset to my brother. When she came in, my brother mentioned that they all needed coffee. She took her pad, and one by one, asked how each would like their coffee. When she finished, she ripped the sheet off her pad, handed it to my brother, and walked out of the room. She may have mumbled something about not being a waitress on her way out. What a fabulous lesson for teaching my brother respect and possibly discrimination.

The average person will always treat management with respect. The "chair" demands respect, whether or not you respect the person. However, you will have to remind yourself occasionally that peers and your subordinates deserve the same respect. Respect for your subordinates is vitally important because your success depends more on your subordinates than anything else. If they are not treated professionally, you will suffer.

If you have a boss, you absolutely cannot respect, do exactly what he says and watch what happens. You will soon have a brand-new boss. Every boss makes mistakes and when you recognize that mistake, but comply, instead of pointing it out, things are not going to go well for your boss. And don't forget that your own employees know that, too.

Cultivate Connections

The old saying: **"It's not what you know, but who you know"** is especially relevant in a corporate environment. Your job will almost always depend on cooperation and help from disciplines outside your area. Knowing someone personally in these other disciplines can result in extra effort when you request their help.

It is much easier to ask a familiar face for a favor than to ask a stranger. But, of course, you must always be willing to reciprocate. Doing a favor for someone else is one of the best ways to cultivate connections. While you do the favor, always try to remember the person's name and responsibility. It not only shows respect but also helps you remember who to call when you need help.

The most important connection to cultivate is your relationship with your mentors. Often, you will not even know who they are. It will usually be someone above you who has been impressed enough with your work that they begin acting as your advocate and advisor. If you discover someone acting in that role for you, do your best to show that you appreciate and deserve their faith in you. Asking their advice is an excellent way to build the relationship while allowing you to view the company from a higher level.

Often a mentor relationship can develop as a result of getting to know the person socially. This is another reason that it is helpful to participate in company-sponsored activities outside of work. It is frequently an activity like golf or community service. For example, one of my important mentor relationships resulted from a chance meeting at a church-sponsored volunteer workday.

Also, don't miss the opportunity to mentor an outstanding subordinate. For example, one employee whom I sponsored for his first management assignment, became my manager some years later. That appreciative relationship was immensely helpful when I needed executive support on staffing new programs and future budgeting requests.

The Boss is Always Right

Remember the Golden Rule: "**He who has the gold makes the rules.**" Or, as my old boss was fond of saying: "You live in a democracy. You don't work in one." So, an astute employee who hopes to move up in an organization should never correct his boss unless he is certain that boss would appreciate it, and not be offended.

Have you ever been in a meeting where someone made a comment, and you found yourself thinking: "He shouldn't have said that." It was a comment that would make the boss look bad, even though it might have been accurate. The point, of course, is to think of what affect the comment could have on your career and how it would impact that person's view of you.

Fred, one of the best engineering managers who reported to me, had a habit of interrupting and correcting anyone who had made a mistake in a meeting. It didn't matter who had made the misstatement; he simply interrupted with a point of correction, regardless of who made the mistake.

After one such meeting, I was called into the general manager's office. He said to me: "Fred is so good; I want you to fire him. I can't stand him." He was serious. It took some wrangling on my part to keep from having to do it. The single characteristic of being so indiscriminately critical kept Fred, one of the most capable managers I ever worked with, from being considered for advancement. It was even jeopardizing his employment.

On another occasion, I was asked to sit in for my boss at the top executive's staff meeting. In the meeting, the company president stood up and started spewing out a train of ideas, some of which I thought were rather bazaar. I remember looking across the table at a VP whom I had known for some time, and wrinkled my brow with a questioning expression. He looked at me and quickly winked. His wink was an acknowledgment that he noticed that I was not speaking up. I understood. No one was challenging any of the points because of fear that it might embarrass the boss. You don't embarrass or correct the boss, especially at that level, and keep your job. Correcting that particular individual could be likened to signing your resignation.

There are certainly times when you can disagree with the boss and feel justified to point out that he is wrong. At these times, you will have a decision to make. Do you point out the mistake and risk his resentment, or let it go and protect your standing? One factor in favor of speaking up is whether the boss could later discover that you knowingly allowed him to make a mistake. If you do decide to speak up, try to do it privately. Your manager may actually appreciate the information.

Choose Your Boss Wisely

Of course, you don't always have a choice of who your boss will be, but "who the boss is" should figure strongly in whether to take a new position. Some bosses tend to pull their "trusted" folks along with them as they move up the ladder. This can be a big plus for you because you will always be one of his "loyal and trusted" employees.

How will you know when your boss is headed up the ladder? Here are a few questions to ask yourself: Does he get picked by *his* boss to sit in when he is away? How well does he seem to work with management?

I once worked for a *Fortune* 500 company in which eight of the 12 on the executive board had belonged to the same college fraternity. It was clear that one exceptionally successful executive had brought his "trusted friends" along with him.

In addition to the benefits of working for a boss who may be destined for advancement, there is also an advantage if you work for someone with a style that is compatible with, or complementary to your own. I noticed an amusing example of this phenomenon once when I was managing a large engineering consulting group. I had made it a practice to have a one-on-one meeting with folks who worked for managers reporting to me. It was called "skip levels." I tried to have several each month, and over a year or so, I became acquainted with folks who worked for the managers reporting to me.

Two of those skip-level interviews provided a clear example of how style compatibility can be a factor in job enjoyment. As I interviewed my first employee in this area, he mentioned that the only thing he disliked was that his boss kept telling him what to do and how to do it. A few months later I was talking with another of that manager's staff, and he mentioned that he especially liked his job because his boss not only told him what to do but also how to do it. That boss's style was a good match for the second employee, but not the first. Both employees were capable contributors, but results will always be greater when the employee is not distracted by compatibility issues.

Don't feel guilty if you find yourself in a group where the boss's style is a big problem for you. Of course, you have to do everything you possibly can to please that boss, but since killing your boss is usually frowned upon, you should also start thinking about making a job change. And don't forget to do exactly what he says.

Know Your Boss and Try to Meet His Needs

Doing a good job is the number one way to meet your boss's needs. However, every manager will have a particular style, and understanding your manager's style can help you meet his needs.

As you prepare to be a better manager yourself, you should certainly seek formal management training. We will discuss this in detail later, but one aspect of that training will include techniques to discover management styles. The Hersey-Blanchard Situational Leadership Model is one of many useful tools that will give insight into your own as well as your boss's dominant style. If you are like me, you will be relieved to discover that there is no best style. Instead, many different supervising styles can become highly effective managers.

The most important aspect of style analysis is to help you better understand yourself as well as your boss. However, even without formal training, you will usually be able to determine the significant aspects of your boss's style. It should be easy to see what is important to him and what his needs are.

One of the most common needs of your boss is time. You can help meet that need by preparing for a session with him. First, practice how you can make your points quickly and get him to the decision point efficiently. Then, try to put yourself in his shoes. What questions is he likely to ask? Do you have the answers? Try to explore all the answers you can before starting the session. If he asks a question, you should know but don't, you should resist the urge to guess. Instead, simply acknowledge the good question and either describe how you will find the answer or simply say you will give him a reply later.

As you learn more about your boss, you can focus on what is most important to him. In one situation, I forced myself to learn how to play golf. My boss had a strong need for building a relationship, and he loved golf. I never learned to love golf the way he did, but it served the purpose at the time. I became closer to my boss by playing golf with him.

That said, you can also be too close to the boss. Sometimes a boss will be reluctant to promote someone who everyone knows to be his best friend. (At least, if the boss is smart, he will be sensitive to that.) Being too close to the boss can hurt your chances for advancement in that case. If you find yourself in the position of being perceived as a close friend of the boss, make certain that boss knows your career goals and aspirations. If he is a good boss, he will always be willing to help you along.

Blend with the Politics and Beliefs

Occasionally your boss, or even company cultures, will be strong advocates of a particular political or religious ideology. Acquiescing to these beliefs is always the wise path for the ambitious employee.

In the span of five years, I worked for two senior executives who seemed to represent the opposite extremes of political thinking. One was the most liberal Democrat you could imagine. He represented Bernie Sanders on steroids. The other, who replaced the Democrat, was the staunchest conservative I have ever seen. He was to the right of Ted Cruz. Both of these men were suspicious of anyone who did not share their views.

As a traditional independent, I was surprised to see that I enjoyed becoming a temporary Democrat and temporary Republican. I learned to lie and promise the absurd with the Democrats and lie and deny basic rights with the Republicans. It helped me survive both administrations. On the other hand, I watched others with strong opposite beliefs suffer as they were reluctant to tolerate such extremes. While working with both political parties, I also learned that all politicians were singularly focused on one thing: getting elected or re-elected. There never seemed to be any personal conviction associated with positions they took on issues. They simply did the things that they felt would get the most votes, which, unfortunately, often meant pleasing the handful of large contributors who made their campaign possible.

Occasionally religious preferences spill over into the workplace as well. Again, the best path is tolerance. Respecting someone's faith is part of respecting the person. Respecting every person is very important. It is also wise not to initiate discussions about religion or politics. The wise move is to simply conform to the politics and beliefs in the workplace. **It is human nature to favor those who think like you do, and your boss is probably human.**

Relationships Are More Important Than Being Right.

Your relationships with peers are almost as important as your relationship with your boss. So, give careful attention to what is worth fighting for and what is not worth fighting for.

It is common in a competitive environment to point out to the boss an error or mistake made by one of your peers. I know it always gave me a good feeling. The boss is always grateful, which makes you think you have moved up a notch in his eyes. After all, you have just shown that you are better than that peer. But don't do it. It will get back to the peer, and you will now have an enemy. Try instead to speak to that person, and one-on-one, address the difference of opinion or mistake.

A peer manager once reported a huge mistake that my group was making to upper management. It was a false accusation that must have been based on a mistaken assumption he had made. Instead of confronting him privately, I waited until the weekly area management meeting and attacked his claim with the facts. I received satisfaction from seeing his red face at the end of the meeting. I had just made a big, big mistake. Our relationship was strained from then on.

The worst part for me was that ten years later, that previous peer became my boss's boss. My immediate boss, who was a friend, once revealed to me that this executive had told him to find a way to fire me. I feel fortunate that he never found the way.

What I should have done when the peer made the initial report was to go to him, one-on-one, with the facts. He could have twisted out of his previous statements and saved face. The lesson I learned was this: Disagreements are almost always a result of misunderstandings. Try to settle disputes with discussions of data rather than counterattacks. And yes, I know this takes all the fun out of work.

Prepare for the Day that Work Ends

Retirement is the best scenario for the end of your employment career. Unfortunately, other circumstances can also result in your loss of regular income. Therefore, you need to prepare for any and all possibilities as you move through your career.

There was a time when companies provided a generous retirement benefit to instill loyalty in employees. That day is gone. However, most companies do provide volunteer savings programs that offer tax savings and often include matching contributions. Participate at the maximum in these programs. Retirement can be the best years of your life, but only if you have prepared financially.

Too often, your loss of income is simply the result of restructuring, downsizing, or outsourcing your job. These times can become a stepping stone to an even better career if you have set aside enough to weather the transition. This sounds like living below your means, but it is not. It is simply adopting the financial discipline necessary to build a buffer. The smart ones who successfully build this buffer invariably keep saving even after they reach their target. The buffer becomes an investment enabler. Those who maintain this discipline, can often become wealthy.

5. BASIC RULES FOR MANAGERS

Obtain Formal Management Training

To be a Leader you must be a Learner. One important reason is that there are subtleties in U.S. labor regulations that you must know to keep from violating the law. A second reason to have formal management training is that you will find that you can be a much more effective manager of people by understanding some of the processes and methods developed by professionals who have dedicated their lives to the art of management. Just as you can learn to be a better public speaker, you can discover techniques that enable you to be a superior manager.

One of the best ways to learn management techniques is through private and professional organizations' many training seminars and courses. Less costly are all the management books and online courses. Each has valuable points and lessons that will improve your abilities. However, resist the lure of thinking that they contain all the keys to successful management. In fact, it is best to avoid courses that claim to have all the answers. (no, this management book does not have "all the keys" either.)

As a final point on management education, make sure you understand your own company's management rules and procedures. For example, every company seems to have a different appraisal and rating system. Although I have never seen a particularly good one, you need to know, and be rigorous in the execution, of your company's system.

In my opinion, the best appraisal system would be one that allows a manager to discuss with the employee strengths, weaknesses, and ways to be an even better contributor without assigning a number or rank to the person. Salary discussions would be separated from that session. Telling any employee where his manager ranks compared to other employees can also have an adverse effect on performance.

When I worked for IBM, it practiced an appraisal system that rated every employee between 5 and 1, with 1 being the best. Ratings in a department were supposed to follow a bell curve, with only 10% receiving the 1 rating. On the other hand, their practice in recruiting was to hire only 3.5 grade-point average or above college graduates. This system had a discouraging effect on employees when they were told that even though they had worked hard to be an "A" student all their lives, they were now a "C" student because only 10% could be "A's". It was impossible to convince them that a "C" was good. What I noticed instead was that they tended to become a "C" employee. (More on this phenomenon in the section on "Expecting employees to be what you want them to be" in chapter 6.)

An interesting anecdote on this subject happened when a group of senior human resources managers at IBM had concluded that the company should change the appraisal system from ten levels to five. It seems that Thomas Watson Jr, the current president, had been intimately involved in creating the system and everyone was reluctant to propose the change. Finally, a meeting was set up with Watson to present the proposal. The amusing thing that happened when they finished the presentation was that Watson stood up and said: "You people have missed the point. It doesn't matter what this format is. The only reason we have this system is to force managers to sit down and talk to employees once a year." Of course, he approved the change, but more importantly, he forced everyone into a new level of thinking.

I never met Watson, but a friend of mine did. My friend was teaching one segment of a class in IBM's Armonk New York training center and began running over on his allotted time. During the break, he had told the regular instructor to call and have the airport limo delay his pick up by an hour. When he finished, he ran out and was relieved to see the limo sitting there. He jumped in the back seat and immediately noticed how nice this airport limo was. It had drinks, a TV and everything. Then he noticed that they had not moved.

He pecked on the window and said: LaGuardia, please. The driver turned around and said: "not unless your name is Tomas J. Watson." Apparently, Watson was meeting some executives at that training center (an imposing place) that day. As my friend's face reddened, he quickly opened the door and started getting out. About that time, Tomas J. opened the other door and sat down. As my friend apologized, Watson interrupted and said: "We can do airport." He then took him all the way to LaGuardia. For me, that was another lesson from this fellow.

Appraise Employees with Fairness and Sensitivity.

Thomas J said it was important to sit down and talk to your employee once a year. It may indeed be the single most important thing you do as a manager. So, be certain to treat it that way. Learn the process and prepare.

The approach I found most useful for me, as well as effective, is a **two-way appraisal.** The employee is asked to identify strengths and weaknesses of me, his manager, as well as suggestions for improvement. I notified the employee of the meeting to discuss these things a week or two ahead to allow them to prepare, just as I was doing. Of course, this assumes that you have completed a performance plan with the employee the year before.

As I was writing the appraisal, I had to remind myself occasionally to focus on employee skills that were important to the job. It is easy to find personal attributes that really do not belong in the discussion. I also found it better to build on what the employee does well instead of correcting areas of weakness. As you include future plans, it is also much better to talk about "goals" rather than "areas for improvement." The key here is to be specific. As a simplified example, don't say "improve punctuality," say "be at work at 7:30," or "finish the project by the second Tuesday of next week". Be specific. During the discussion, I found it helpful to identify one thing that would help the employee and me to be more productive.

Real improvement can happen by focusing on building on strengths along with having the session a two-way discussion. I felt like I became a better manager, and the employee became more productive. I also found that I learned things about the employee that I didn't know. Often these things allowed me to see the "why" of someone's skills. When you have a more thorough knowledge of employees, you can be a better manager for them. In addition, it can help you target assignments they are more likely to enjoy and excel in, while building on their skills.

Also, this performance discussion is a great time to include plans for training and education. An education or training plan can help turn any areas that need improvement into a positive. By offering to do something yourself, in this case, arrange training, you assume some responsibility for the weakness. This technique not only softens the criticism, but allows the employee to embrace the plan for improvement.

I think most managers are like me and hate to do appraisals. It is difficult to make this a positive experience for the employee and ensure you have pointed out weaknesses as well as strengths. This is undoubtedly why appraisals frequently miss the scheduled dates. Nevertheless, this is very important work for a manager and requires your best effort.

Understand all Aspects of Your Area

You cannot make good decisions about your area if you do not fully understand what your area does, how it is done, and its importance to the business.

The corporation where I worked once transferred a vice president to take over the highly technical division to replace a recently retired executive. The new VP's background had been exclusively in nontechnical administration. He quickly made a few changes in the accounting area that seemed to have positive results. However, it became evident that he didn't understand the technology behind our final product. He frequently focused attention on trivial items while ignoring issues that could significantly impact our business. He simply did not understand the difference between the two. He didn't understand our business. That lack of understanding caused him to make bad decisions much too often.

If you take over your boss's position, you probably already know the business. However, if the area is new to you, spend much of your initial effort learning the business. Understanding the processes and the people is the best thing you can do in the first six months of a new job (Much more on this subject in the chapter on becoming a management professional.)

Address Accusations of Misconduct Promptly
(Where there is smoke, there is fire.)

One of the managers reporting to me came into my office one day and mentioned that a female employee had complained to him about sexual harassment from another employee in her department. She accused him of walking up behind her as she sat in her office and rubbing her back. The manager doubted that the accusation had much foundation because of his history with that female employee. It seems she had a history of making complaints to him about little things going on all the time. She also didn't have the kind of "catch your eye" appearance that would have been associated with attracting most men. Nevertheless, the manager had confronted the accused employee and received the response that she had simply misrepresented his simple friendliness.

I told the manager to have another talk with the accused employee and tell him that the lady was sensitive and that his "misinterpreted friendliness" could not be tolerated. Have him stay away from the lady. Maybe that solved the issue. I forgot about it until about a year and a half later when the company had a major downsizing and lots of folks elected to take the generous retirement package the company offered. On the day of the scheduled exit of all the new retirees, one of those leaving who happened to be in that lady's department stuck his head into my office and asked if I had a minute. As he sat down, he said he had something to get off his chest before he left the company. He asked if I remembered the sexual harassment instance. He wanted to tell me the rest of the story. He related that as his office was across the hall, he had not only seen the incident, but he had also seen many more. He said that this man was not rubbing her back; he was reaching around and rubbing her front. He had seen this and other related behaviors more than once from that man.

What an eye-opener. I had made a huge mistake. If I had investigated the incident instead of pushing it aside, I would have discovered not only how serious the problem was but that this man had exhibited a pattern of inappropriate behavior. Now it was too late. Both employees had left the company. I did realize that the lady may have achieved exactly what she desired, which was no more contact. This motive would explain her softening of the accusation. However, I missed the opportunity to do the right thing by ensuring zero tolerance of harassment.

About a year later, one of my managers mentioned in an "oh, by the way" comment that a woman on one of the production assembly lines had complained about her line supervisor acting inappropriately toward her. He said that it didn't make much sense to him and that he had discounted the complaint. What a red flag that was for my "learned my lesson" brain. I told him to arrange one-on-one interviews for me with every woman on that assembly line.

I had a bit of trouble executing my plan as the first woman I talked with seemed too nervous to want to be open with me. I wasn't making any accusations about any problems; I was just trying to get a feeling for the atmosphere on that assembly line. Then, during the woman No. 8 interview, I hit pay dirt. This woman was not nervous at all and right away dove into a problem with their supervisor. It seemed that she felt sorry for this pretty girl on the line, who the supervisor could not keep his hands off. More confirmations of the harassment soon came forth. Finally, the supervisor actually admitted his problem, but that didn't save his job.

The point, of course, is to investigate any and all claims of misconduct. Not only are you at risk of violating labor laws if you don't, but you also risk disrespecting your employees. Everyone deserves respect.

These were obvious examples of harassment. However, harassment can also be subtle and depend on the interpretation of the person involved. There was this delightful older lady who was single who was always dressed nicely but often somewhat provocatively. She always seemed to be flirting with younger men. One morning as I got out of my car in the parking lot, I noticed her exiting her car. As she started walking to the door, I gave a quick wolf whistle in her direction. She shook a little and began to walk with more than a little strut, twisting from side to side. I think I made her day.

However, after about three paces, I stopped dead in my tracks and looked around—anyone who would have seen that could have interpreted it as sexual harassment. I could have just lost my job. Needless to say, I never did that again. Harassment can be that innocent.

Avoid Discrimination

I have never met anyone who didn't harbor some level of prejudice. Scientific studies have shown that we are born with it. Babies smile when they see a baby that looks like themselves and tend to crawl toward them. They crawl away from a baby who looks different than them. If we are all born with this trait, then each manager must consciously work to avoid every type of discrimination - age, sex, national heritage, religion, or appearance.

Once, when my business area in a big company was closing down, I began interviewing for other jobs in the same company. One of the openings that I was most interested in was an engineering management position. During my interview with the VP decision-maker, I found myself wishing I had brought a tape recorder. I thought that because the VP said he knew he could not find anyone more qualified or capable for this position, but "frankly," he said, "I am looking to put a younger person into the job." (Right now, I find my fingers trying to type his name, but I won't let them. ... Sometimes you have to discipline your fingers just like your tongue.) I often wondered if he realized what a blatant example of age discrimination he had demonstrated. (No, I didn't get the job.)

Many years ago, my boss, who was a senior manager, came into my office with a large stack of résumés and told me he wanted me to sort this stack down to a handful for him to review. He said that the first cut he wanted me to make was to pull out everyone over 40. That was clearly age discrimination.

On another occasion, the company I worked for was found to be in non-compliance with the standards for the percent of females and minorities in engineering and management jobs. As a result, a memo was sent to all management saying that, for the foreseeable future, every new hire and promotion would be female or minority. This was going to be difficult because at that time, the pool of women and minorities graduating from college with technical degrees was such a small percent of total graduates. The university where I had attended was predominantly an engineering school and had only one female in the freshman class. A change came over time, but that was the environment at that time. To guarantee female engineering hires, the starting pay was raised to a much higher figure than the existing staff was making. As time passed, the follow-on promotions became known as token managers, as many were ineffective in that role. That seemed to be reverse discrimination, and it probably reinforced prejudice for some in the majority because many of the beneficiaries were ineffectual.

Fortunately, the years of blatant discrimination and overcompensation are largely behind us. Many years after that adjustment period, I found myself doing engineering kickoff meetings at a major university. It was interesting to see that the last time I spoke to a freshman class, white males were a minority. It was refreshing to see that the focus on this subject in America had paid off.

In an earlier section, I mentioned a recommendation to conform to dress and appearance norms. However, as a manager, you will have to guard against judging employees based on appearance, language proficiency, or anything unrelated to the job. Of course, there are exceptions, such as expecting a salesman to represent your company professionally. Again, however, you will have to consciously guard against any prejudice that you may not even be aware of.

What do you think of when someone tells you where they went to school? Was that a prejudiced thought? It was for me. I went to four different universities before I escaped. Some were better than others. Therefore, I just naturally think of someone from the better school as better. I am consequently prejudiced and have to guard against that.

Enormous progress has been made in the recognition of, and actions to prevent discrimination in America. However, I do not believe we will ever completely eliminate the inherent prejudices that exist. For that reason, a manager must be especially diligent in ensuring that it does not happen in the workplace. Therefore, it is essential that managers have training in this field, understand relevant regulations, and be alert for problematic situations that may arise.

Cultivate a Few Trusted Critics

As you move up in an organization, colleagues are often reluctant to point out your errors and mistakes. It is not a good practice to correct the boss, which means that your employees will be reluctant counselors. Peers are not motivated to point out your mistakes either, as your mistakes make them look better in comparison. But a mistake can ruin your career. Having a trusted critic or two can save the day for you.

I have a habit of making little jokes when I am around people, and too often in business meetings. It seems that these funny things or twists of someone's comments just come into my head, and I share them. Sometimes, people laugh. It is a bad habit.

In one particular meeting that I don't like to remember, I was making a presentation, and I made one of my comments, and a few people laughed. I continued with the meeting without thinking any more about the joke. Then, after the meeting, a friend came into the office and made me aware that my comment would have been offensive to anyone of Chinese descent. There were two employees from China in the meeting. It was an insight that never occurred to me at all. Realizing my inappropriate behavior, I apologized individually to each attendee at the meeting. I have since tried to think before blurting out something that I think is funny. I wish it always worked.

Just as my friend may have saved me future embarrassment, having a trusted friend can help you salvage a bad situation or mistake you have made. Developing a path for this type of help is to seek out feedback from a respected friend. This is best accomplished with the person one-on-one. You will probably have to be the initiator for the feedback until the relationship develops. Then, one day he will walk into your office and say, "Boss, did you really mean to say this in the staff meeting?" That will be the day that he will save your bacon.

There's a funny story about how that fellow became a trusted friend. It seems that we were both fresh out of college and beginning our first professional jobs. After a brief orientation on my first day, the HR person took me to a private office I would be sharing with another engineer. Soon after I had commandeered the best desk, the HR person showed up with another new employ, and my office mate.

My new office mate simply stood in the door and looked at me. He was a thin fellow and wore cowboy boots that seemed to come up to his ears. After a minute of looking at me he said: "I like harses," which I was pretty sure meant horses. I looked back at him and said, "I like harses too." He said, "we're going to get along." And we did get along. He was a good engineer and very helpful. The only difficulty for me was that he did want to talk about horses a lot.

I would listen to his horse stories and felt compelled to share my own stories. The problem was that I had never been on a horse. Thankfully, I could remember a number of horse stories that my dad had told, many of them quite interesting about riding here and there. Plagiarizing these stories for my own, gave me something to relate that he seemed to enjoy. In fact, we were getting along so well that he invited me to spend our Thanksgiving holiday on his family's ranch 200 miles away. He badgered me so often on this that I finally relented and agreed to the trip.

It was late when we arrived, and I was really impressed with the enormous house and farmlands. After breakfast he announced to his mother that we were going riding. I felt like our friendship was about to end as I followed him out into the field. After opening the gate to the field, he told me to wait there at the fence. As I waited, he took off up a hill. Soon he returned sitting atop the largest black horse I have ever seen. It had no saddle, just that thing in its mouth. He said, "climb the fence and jump on the back". I did that and tried not to hold too tightly to his back side. The horse walked us down the road about a half mile and my friend said, "Jump off and open the gate and we'll ride." Well, I thought we had been riding, but I jumped off and opened the gate.

As soon as the gate was open, he took off flying over the hill and out of sight. After about 5 or 10 minutes they came galloping back. When he was about stopped, he jumped off and said: "Your turn." I had seen him grab the bridle or reins or whatever, jump on, and swing his leg over, so I tried the same. I almost made a perfect mount with my leg across when the horse took off running. As he went over the hill, I realized that this horse seemed to be going faster than any motorcycle I had ever owned. The problem for me that my only hand that had any part of that bridle was also holding a big wad of neck horse hair. I couldn't pull up on it. I suddenly remembered my dad saying some of his horses would respond to verbal commands, gee, haw, and saugers. I screamed them all, but mostly whoa! Nothing worked. At one point, we were coming up on a fence and he just veered and just keep going top speed. The next thing I saw was the bottom of the hill and a dried-up creek bed. It was about fifteen feet across and three feet deep.

My next memory is waking up on the other side of that creek, noticing that I had trouble standing and had a hand full of horse hair. I finally got up and made my way over to the other side of the creek where the horse was lazily eating grass. I grabbed the bridle again and as I tried to jump up, the horse reached around and bit me on the butt. Thankfully my friend showed up around then. He said I was riding good. I said the horse didn't seem to want to jump the creek. He just looked at me, but we were still friends. The next day in church with his family, I had to sit with a pronounced lean because of my blue back side. Now, I am not saying that you have to learn to ride a horse to develop a trusted friend, but it worked for me.

Never Threaten Employees

The quickest way for a manager to achieve what he wants is to threaten employees. "If you don't do this, this way, I will fire you." I know that there will be times when this might be appropriate, but those times should be exceedingly rare.

I was working for IBM at a time when they were one of the largest customers of GE plastics. As a manager in plastics at our company, I had lunch a few times with Jack Welch, who was then the GE president. In the first discussion I had with him, he immediately opened the subject of what we needed to do to fix our company. He said that we needed to rank our people and lay off the bottom 20% every year.

Can you imagine what kind of environment that plan would create in a company? Everyone would constantly be afraid they would lose their job. So instead of helping each other with work, they would always want to make other workers look incompetent.

A few years later, I found myself in the opposite role dealing with GE. I was the salesman rather than the customer because we supplied electronic components to the Appliance Division of GE. As I became friends with many of the employees, I was told that they did indeed practice an annual ranking to lay off the bottom 10% every year. The atmosphere was extremely stressful for employees. It also forced a continuous kowtowing to the bosses who did the ranking.

A wonderful contrast to that philosophy was being practiced by IBM when I joined them. In my first week of employment as a professional, I attended many meetings. What mystified me was that I could never tell who the boss was in a meeting. That was very unusual. In my previous corporate experiences, even though I didn't know any of the players, I could easily tell who was in charge. Everyone always played up to that person, waiting for his comments and opinions.

At IBM it was simply not the case. People didn't play to the boss because the culture didn't require it. There were several reasons for this open culture. First, at that time, IBM simply didn't lay off employees, except in extremely rare circumstances. That fact eliminated the fear associated with making an offending comment. In one of those early meetings where discussions had become heated, a manager interrupted with a comment: "Could we pause and let the head of our division make a comment?" The participants were ignoring the boss.

Second, the monetary incentive to move up the corporate ladder was not the same as at other companies. At IBM you could make just as much money and have just as lovely an office being a single contributor as you could as a top manager. It was a plan called the parallel career path.

Managers in that environment tended to be coaches rather than dictators. It was a wonderful environment and achieved impressive results. It resulted in the kind of "group think" plans and decisions that yield better solutions. Employees also tended to have a

Robert Vines

personal "buy-in" to work plans. When employees have that kind of buy-in, they always work harder to achieve positive results.

The late Jack Welch had demonstrated an example of a top manager that was recommending the actions of what I call, a jerk. I suppose an astute manager would listen to his advice. Indeed, if you worked at GE, it would have been your only choice. However, if you want the best results and team effort, never create a threatening environment.

Tell Employees What is Needed, Not What you Want

Sometimes Not Getting What You Want is a Wonderful Stroke of Luck – (Dala Lama)

When you tell subordinates exactly what you want them to do, you will get just what you ask for, but you may not get what you need. The employee is not required to use his brain. When that employee sees a potential problem with your specified action, he may not speak up. He might even take a sinister satisfaction in seeing the problem with your instructions and enjoy watching negative results develop.

Instead, tell employees what is needed. Then, let them be a part of determining the solution. The best instruction will include why it is needed. You will be surprised at how many times you will find employees contributing a better way to satisfy that need. You will also be surprised to see how much more effective an employee works when he has a stake in what is being accomplished.

I consulted for a successful entrepreneur for a few years who always kept his business plans close to the vest. He always told us specifically what he wanted us to do. At least, he told us the first step. As I always wanted to exceed his expectations, I would try to do more than he asked. I would anticipate why he needed the information and provide much more data. Invariably, the result would be that he discounted the extra work, telling me just enough to show that what I had done was in the wrong direction. Still, he never told me what he needed and why he needed it.

That strategy worked well in his role as a salesman. Potential customers always felt that his "close to the vest" style was a way of protecting trade secrets that were of immense value. The customer's imagination would feed their expectations of how doing business with this mysterious entrepreneur might be a compelling differentiator for their company. Investing in this entrepreneur's business would likewise be rewarded with substantial gains.

However, that strategy was a lousy management philosophy. It created an environment of trial and error wrapped around his thinking alone. If he was not in the office, work tended to stop. Had he simply explained the final goal, instead of a single activity, much more would have been achieved. Of course, presenting the final destination means that the manager has to do the strategic planning necessary to chart a logical path. Doing that strategic planning is a much better use of a manager's time than designing every task.

Terminate With Cause.

There are two fundamental reasons for terminating an employee, violating a condition of employment (i.e., failure to follow company policy), and unsatisfactory performance. Terminating an employee for violating a condition of employment is usually the easy one. The employee did something that cannot be tolerated and must suffer the consequences. In that instance, the prime concern for the manager is ensuring that he is following legal, as well as policy guidelines during the process. Hopefully, you will have a human resources professional to help ensure proper documentation and steps are taken.

I can tell you from personal experience that when you have the actual interview with the employee, you need to remember to say two words: "You're fired." The point is, that this is not a time to beat around the bush. Any attempt to be diplomatic can result in a possible misunderstanding by the employee. Do not say things like, "we find it necessary to replace you or eliminate your work." Simply say, "I have to inform you that effective today, you're fired."

Terminating an employee for performance is less straightforward. It is also more difficult for the manager because he can easily view the problem as a failure of his management ability. As with any termination, this is certainly another instance where a human resources professional can assist. There are state and federal regulations along with your own company policies that must be followed. Most require documented counseling with a progression of performance assessments. It is important the employee know the measurements as well as the consequences and that the employee signs the assessment documents.

I was dealing with a performance problem once where I had concluded that the company would be money ahead by asking the employee to stay home instead of coming to work. He caused so much dissension that he was affecting the performance of the entire group. And, I did feel I had failed to achieve improvement or a better fit for this employee. Fortunately, I had great support from an HR professional to get rid of this employee.

In every case, being fired will be very upsetting for the employee, and you need to be prepared to deal with any possibility that the news might bring. It is often advisable to have another manager present at the time. With one employee, I chose to have security guards nearby. Each situation will be different, depending on your assessment of the employee. Besides always being upsetting to the employee, it will also be upsetting to you. And if it is not upsetting for you, then you don't belong in management.

6. FOCUS ON EMPLOYEES

Find the Right Jobs for Your Employees

Everyone is a genius. But if you judge a fish by its ability to climb a tree, it will live its life thinking it is stupid. (Albert Einstein)

Most employees will say that they are skilled at what they do and are also doing a good job. What you discover as a manager is that each employee tends to be better at some things than others. So, your job is to find out what each person really does do well and see if you can design their job around those abilities.

I once inherited the job of managing a group of process engineering experts. Our job was to solve problems in plastics injection molding plants. The outgoing manager told me that I would probably need to get rid of one of the newer engineers who performed poorly. Right away, I noticed that one reason that he was ineffective was that he spent all his time fooling with his computer instead of being out in the factory where his job was.

I started asking him computer-related questions and soon realized that this engineer was a real computer whiz. I wrestled for a few weeks with this predicament without actually coming up with a way to modify his job. Eventually, I had a meeting with him to discuss the subject and learned that he had a great idea that would solve my problem. He had a dream of a way to add a computer process control system to every injection molding press that could be accessed remotely by every engineer at their desk. I was intrigued by the plan and approved it as a significant project for him. The result was so successful that he received a promotion. A bonus for me was the recognition I received by helping to present this new innovation to the multiple sites of the entire company.

Creating a good match for individual skills is usually not that easy. The real challenge is figuring out where folks excel and tweaking the job to take advantage of those skills. In addition, some employees will require specific training and development before they can become peak contributors.

One of the best approaches for finding the right place for employees was at the sizeable automotive manufacturer where I worked during college. Every new engineer at that company was required to spend their first two years training before being given a permanent assignment. The training consisted of working six months in each of their four major areas for engineers. The company used this type of program for every professional area (accounting, marketing, engineering, etc.).

That automotive company's strategy was one of the best for helping employees find areas where they could develop a passion for their work. It also solved one of the problems in big organizations. Big companies tend to develop into silo structures, with employees often spending their entire careers in one specialty. When that occurs, there is little understanding of what goes on outside their area or how their job affects everyone else. For example, it is not uncommon in many product-oriented companies to see an initial product design that cannot be economically manufactured. Although the design might meet the functional requirements, traditional high-volume manufacturing would be impossible. Cross training every new engineer helped solve that problem for my automotive company.

The training also tended to minimize the bureaucratic barriers that can frustrate employees when they need cooperation from sister areas. Once, when I had a rushed job assignment, I needed another area to complete all the paperwork so that I could move on with my task. Their area had full control of that paperwork, which meant that I could not go forward until they did their part. When they told me I would have to get in line because they were more than a week behind, I simply completed their task myself. I had worked there while in training and knew all the procedures.

That automotive company's process for new employees was the best I have ever seen. Everyone learned the big picture, their job's place in that big picture, and an appreciation for the complexities in areas other than their own. But, of course, another benefit is that it helped the company find the best fit for new employees and the area where they might have the best chance of developing a passion for their work.

Make Training a Part of Every Employee's Job

In today's fast-moving environment, it is impossible to underestimate the benefit of regular training for employees. It is the best way to ensure that your company is competitive and efficient.

My dad told me a meaningful story once about his first company, the Norfolk and Western Railway. He said that there was always an annual employee meeting around Christmas each year. Invariably someone would be recognized during the event for service to the company if they were retiring at the end of the year. That year an old fellow named Wilber was retiring with 50 years' service.

The vice president called Wilber up for the presentation, but before presenting it asked old Wilber what his job was. Wilber nervously replied that he was a "wheel banger." That title was obviously confusing to the VP, so he followed up with another question: "So, Wilber, what does a wheel banger do?" Wilber said that his father had gotten him the job at age 16. When he showed up, the foreman told him to take this little hammer and walk down the length of the train and bang on every wheel of every car. Now, the VP was really confused, so he asked the third question: "And why did you bang on the wheels?" Wilber replied: "I don't know."

Now, every engineer would tell you that when you bang on the steel wheel it will ring and sound like a bell. If the wheel is cracked (an occasional problem on train wheels that can cause the wheel to fail), instead of ringing like a bell, it will go "thud." Every engineer knows that, but Wilber didn't. He had never been trained.

The best training for employees is the on-the-job training they get with help from other employees. As a manager, you need to make sure the more experienced people know that a part of their job is to train new people. Then, when you see results, you also need to recognize the trainer.

New techniques and technologies are surfacing every day. Staying in front of these new developments can give your company a competitive edge. One way to stay in front is to spend money on seminars and conventions. Sponsoring this training also builds appreciation and loyalty for employees. Another way is to encourage research on problems and processes underway in your company.

At one of the small companies where I consulted, the top manager discouraged formal training. He was concerned that employees would leave for better jobs if they had more skills. That company will always be small.

One final point on training: Don't forget your own training needs. I have been fortunate that the companies I worked for always allowed and encouraged training for me. One benefit I consistently discovered was that the training allowed me to view my work from a different level. In the daily grind, I was too occupied to think about the big picture or the strategic direction we were headed. Separated from this everyday work, I not only picked up pointers on something new to me, but I also had time to think. Sometimes the thinking was during a boring seminar, but whatever the reason, it triggered an idea about my normal job. I can remember several times when those thoughts resulted in a new idea or approach for improving processes in my area of responsibility, or how I function personally. One of these epiphanies resulted in a new way for me to structure my own work for meeting deadlines.

Hire a Bell Ringer

Farmers always put effort into determining which cow to hang the bell on to bring the rest of the cows in from the field for milking or feeding. Having a "bell ringer" in a department will pull the rest of the group along and keep the work going. It is amazing to see how the enthusiasm of one very dedicated employee spills over to all the people around him.

The "bell ringer" I remember most was Jasen. Two weeks after my area was closed down, which moved Jasen to another area, his new boss asked for a meeting with me. When the new boss came in for the meeting, he said he had a question to ask, "How do I manage Jasen?" I laughed and told him to stand back and watch but try not to let Jasen kill himself on the job. Sometimes I thought Jasen was going to do just that. He worked so hard on every task that I found myself frequently telling him to go to lunch or go home. He was just so dedicated that he could not seem to stop.

Almost everything Jasen did invariably involved others who worked in the same area. It always seemed that his enthusiasm was infectious. Everyone else would eventually ramp up their work to match his. Before long, I was telling everyone to stop work and go to lunch. When people are working like that, magic can happen. The job gets done better and faster than you could have ever expected. Jasen just had this unique attitude that did not include failure. And one person with that attitude can change a department.

Attitude always seems to be what sets outstanding employees apart. You can train to develop skills, but you will have a particularly challenging time changing attitudes. Determining attitude is also the most elusive trait to assess in your management role of interviewing candidates. I usually ask open-ended questions. "What did you, or do you, like about your current job?" "What do you dislike about that job?" I don't really listen to the first answer. The second answer can be revealing. Someone with a negative attitude will talk for a long time about the second question.

You like to see someone who turns the second question into a positive one by saying how he overcame a bad situation and turned it into an advantage. That applicant is someone with a "can-do" attitude. If the applicant has that attitude and has demonstrated dedication to his commitments, he can be the person that sets the culture in a department. He can be a department "bell ringer."

Of course, you can have negative "bell ringers" who pull a group down. You can try to turn them around, but the best thing to do is to rid your team of them. Let them take someone else's cows in the wrong direction. The old saying that **"progress follows the Hurst"** is also true for a negative "bell ringer."

Finally, every employee you hire may not be a bell ringer, but the focus on all hiring should still emphasize attitude. Several years ago, when General Motors was a dominant US company, they surveyed the backgrounds of their management. What they discovered surprised everyone. The employees who continually rose in the organization tended not to be the 4.0 graduates but the average to slightly above average graduates. It was the C+ and B students who advanced in the organization. As they looked further, they found that it was the students who were involved in other activities on campus, and often paying their own way in school.

This result emphasizes the importance of looking past grades as you interview candidates. Look instead for evidence of areas where they demonstrated initiative. Did they hold an office in social or other organizations? Did they contribute to, or pay for their education? It is always a plus if there is evidence that they got along well with peers because so much of their success at work will depend on working with others. Ask about their outside interests just as you will about their related job experience.

Also, remember that with today's labor regulations, the only time you can easily fire a person is the day you are interviewing them for the job. So put real effort into these choices. Your management training will also help you learn techniques for interviewing.

The most important of those techniques is listening instead of talking during the interview. An interview should be a two-way conversation. A prepared candidate will have good questions. And when you ask a question, a good candidate will not feel awkward about pausing to reflect before answering. Listening sounds easy to do, but it is not. After all, you are proud of what you offer in a job and want to sell it to the candidate. Instead, avoid the sales pitch and listen.

Expect Employees to Be what you Want Them to Be

People respond better to positive reinforcement than to negative criticism. I was once staffing an important new program at IBM and was told by executive management that I could conscript anyone I wanted in the company. I had a real advantage at that time because I had worked as a non-manager peer alongside many of the potential candidates. So, of course, I picked many of the top-rated folks from other groups to be a part of our team. But one engineer didn't fit that model. This engineer was simply someone that I felt was better than his poor rating indicated.

A surprising thing happened when he was being transferred to my team. During the required appraisal prior to the transfer, his manager gave him the top rating of a "1," which raised his appraisal by two numbers. I knew what that manager was trying to do. He resented giving up any of his people and was setting me up for a bad situation. As you could only have 10% of a group rated a "1," I would have to drop this engineer's rating at his next appraisal, which would make for an unhappy employee and a little revenge for the previous manager.

During that next year, before his first appraisal, an interesting thing happened. This engineer became a "1." He had been told that he was one of the absolute best, and that is what he became. He certainly changed. He began taking the lead, working late, and being twice as effective as I had ever seen before. He had become one of our "bell ringers."

What I learned in that experience was that people tend to become what you expect them to be. Or, as Max Planck famously said, **"When you change the way you look at things around you, the things around you change."**

I also discovered that it was better to praise someone for something that he needed improvement in rather than criticize him. For example, there was this one employee who was consistently disruptive in meetings. Anytime I mentioned something on the subject to him, I always got a response that seemed to be defensively attacking me or the particular circumstance I was using as an example. So, finally, I tried a different approach with him than the usual reprimand. I told him how much I appreciated his ability to let others talk, considering their points before speaking. Almost immediately, I noticed him sitting quietly in meetings, thinking about what to say next. He had never seemed to listen or let others explain their point before speaking up in the past. It was a perfect example of having behavior change to meet expectations.

Psychologists tell us that a person who is the recipient of acts of kindness will perform charitable acts in return. That phenomenon can be a useful management tool. In my example, my act of kindness was the compliment I was paying the employee. His act in return was to not interrupt others as quickly in meetings. Never pass up an opportunity to do an act of kindness for an employee. Other employees may benefit from your thoughtfulness. Being altruistic pays off.

Recognition of a job well done can also be the biggest acts of kindness a manager can give to an employee. This same thinking applies to yourself. As Henry Ford is credited to have said: **"Whether you think you can, or whether you think you can't; you're right."** It is not just important to believe your employees can; you must believe that you can. Choose your words carefully, especially when you are talking to yourself. Words like "if only," "I can't," and "I must" can keep you from taking action. Try to replace these words with "let's look at this another way," "I will," and "I choose to." When disaster strikes, replace "why me" with "what can I do about this." It will inspire a sense of strength, pointing you toward corrective action rather than blaming others for your problems.

Recognize Accomplishments and Always Credit Effort

Success in any project is often beyond the control of any single individual regardless of his effort. However, if you do not give credit for effort in times of failure, you will never get the level of effort you need so that employees are inspired to continue to push projects until they succeed.

One of the worst bosses I ever worked for (Lloyd) had a way of killing incentive in employees better than anyone I have ever seen. He was an Army-commander-style manager. Behind his desk, he had pinned about 20 3x5 cards on the wall with sayings indicating his management philosophy. I remember one in particular that said: "No Credit for Effort."

On one particularly difficult product startup, a problem developed one evening that would prevent the normal start of production the next day. One of my employees stayed in the factory all night working on a solution. By 6:00 a.m. he had found a solution. It allowed us to start production on time and kept us from sending 400 employees home.

I was so proud of him that I took him in to see the "big boss," Lloyd. I wanted him to get the recognition that he deserved. Lloyd looked at my sleepy employee after I had told the story and said, "you lucky bastard." That comment completely deflated my employee.

Instead of complimenting his hard work, Lloyd had called it luck. There may have been some luck involved, but there was also a lot of effort and hard work.

I didn't take any more employees in to see Lloyd. But I did take the time to copy down those sayings behind his desk and make up a set for myself. I turned each one around just a little, like "Credit for Effort." Those cards became some of my better management lessons. But, of course, I waited until I was working for a new manager before putting them on the wall.

I had another boss who seemed to criticize everything. I don't think I ever saw him pass along a compliment. Once, after working long and hard on a big project, I made a presentation to him. As I left his office, I realized that he had asked some questions but never said something negative or critical. I took that as the only compliment I ever received from him. Of course, he may have been distracted with some other urgent matter, but I sure felt good.

One final suggestion on recognizing effort and accomplishments: It is easy to appear superior when complimenting an employee. Using the wrong words can turn a comment into a condescending or patronizing statement. Your goal is to appreciate the action and hard work, not to judge the person. Talk about the achievement, not the person. Instead of saying: "you are brilliant," say: "what an accomplishment. You must have worked extremely hard." In that example, saying he is brilliant is judgmental, which positions you as superior. If he feels "brilliant," he no longer has to work hard to meet requirements. If his hard work resulted in his success, he is more likely to work even harder.

Remember, to avoid any misunderstanding, always think about what you are planning to say and how it could be misconstrued before passing along the compliment. Your compliment should be stating an observation and not judgmental. When you are being judgmental, you are setting yourself up as superior. You may be his manager, but you are not his superior.

Discipline Employees with Delicacy and Diplomacy

It is human nature to avoid confrontation. A good manager must overcome that lure and confront unacceptable behavior immediately. It is best done in private and with significant forethought.

When giving direct criticism is the appropriate action for an employee, it is always better to separate the problem from the person. Never criticize the person. Criticize the behavior or the situation. You may have concluded that the employee is slow or lazy. For example, you have observed that the employee has a problem meeting deadlines. That conclusion was your opinion, not a fact. Likewise, you do not know what is in an employee's mind or where he has been. You have not lived in their shoes.

Therefore, your observations are the only thing you can talk about to the employee. Then, you can discuss actions to improve that observation. And, the key, is to make that a discussion. In the discussion, you may discover reasons for the problem and be able to work with the employee to put together actions for improvement. You may also discover a personal tragedy or situation that explains the behavior, especially if you have noticed a performance change. Above all, be timely with this discussion. Do not wait until an annual appraisal or a future session. Instead, act with forethought, but have the discussion as quickly as possible, while it is fresh in your mind.

It is even better to personalize the problem by telling him how his action made you feel. Then, the problem becomes yours, not theirs. The bonus comes when he realizes that he can fix your problem.

I had an employee once who seemed to be disparaging one group or other in meetings constantly. If it weren't the Democrats that caused the problem, it would be management. I had occasionally confronted that employee by attacking the facts in what he had said. What I got in response was an argument as he defended his statement. We usually parted, agreeing to disagree.

Finally, one day I brought him into my office and told him how it made me feel when he did that. It hurt my feelings because I found myself in that category of scoundrel that he had talked about that day. He tried to say that he did not mean to include me. I then reminded him of another instance where he seemed to want to offend anyone from the South. From his lack of argument, I could tell that he was beginning to understand what I was talking about. A couple of weeks later, I noticed he began to comment and then started looking around the room. I was imagining that he was thinking about whom he might offend. Maybe it was because of our conversation.

7. MANAGE WITH EXCELLENCE

Delegate Effectively

When a subordinate steps into your office and presents you with a problem, resist the temptation to fix that problem for him. **When you take responsibility for someone, you take responsibility away from someone.** Lyndon Johnson would often say, "Employees need to feel that it is their own interest to make you look good by doing a good job." Assuming responsibility for a subordinate's job will remove his self-interest.

I had a boss once whom I loved. When I had a problem with getting something done, I would always take it to him. As soon as I finished with my statement of the problem, he would immediately do one of two things. He would either pick up the phone and call someone to help, or he would tell me what he was going to do to help me fix my problem. It was a wonderful environment for me. I never had a problem. My boss always took them away from me. Of course, an additional issue almost always resulted because my boss rarely solved my problems on time. At least, I always had someone to blame.

A technique that worked for me when a subordinate comes in with a problem, was to simply say: "Boy, I am going to be interested in how you are going to solve this. A smart fellow like you will probably end up with some really creative solution. Keep me posted."

Of course, I always asked questions, and occasionally I could help without getting involved or taking too much of my time, but I tried to never take the problem away from him.

New managers often have difficulty delegating. After all, the new manager was likely put into the job because he knew how to do things better than anyone else. He probably can fix that problem more quickly and effectively than the subordinate. What he must realize is that fixing the problem is not what he is being paid to do.

Never Act on Only One Version of a Story.

There will be times when an employee comes into your office and spews out a terrible story about something that had just happened. It will sound so awful you will want to do something immediately to take care of the problem. Resist that urge. Instead, collect more information.

I once worked at a campus of factories that depended on one dedicated group of utilities buildings that contained compressors and HVAC units etc. A central control building controlled everything. One morning, an overly dramatic manager of that center reported to the site general manager that an overload was about to occur, which would shut down the entire complex in four hours.

The site general manager activated our emergency crisis-management process, which triggered a "stop everything" status throughout the complex. In minutes, a war room was set up with arrangements underway to evacuate 4,000 employees.

I had managed that maintenance group in the past and remembered the key technical guy who had led the design of that central system. He worked for the original construction contractor. I gave him a call. After I told him about our problem, he laughed. He said that the main control sometimes lost itself and gave that kind of error. He said that all we needed to do was switch to manual mode and reboot the main control system. I made that suggestion to one of the supervisors in the control building.

The maintenance supervisor credited the miracle fix to his competent staff as he reported the good news to his overly dramatic boss. That boss, of course, took full credit for saving the day when he reported the good news to the site manager. There was no reason for me to clarify that. (Notice how I had finally learned my lesson.)

The real problem in that scenario is that the site general manager reacted based on one story from one person. Instead, he should have asked questions and looked for confirmation of the facts before acting.

Having made similar mistakes of acting too quickly, I learned to say, **"Show me."** It is surprising to see how many times the story changes when you do your own analysis of the situation. Sometimes a simple walk around is all it takes to defuse a fear or first impression.

Take a Break

Creative thinking happens when you interrupt the daily grind by attending a trade show or having an offsite brainstorming session. Sometimes it is an inspiration from a motivational speaker—other times just a simple thought that comes to you as you seek new ideas in a brainstorming session. That new thought can often point your business in a better direction. It is at these times that you can best set the framework for strategic planning.

Your daily routine at the workplace is usually filled with tactical obligations and short-term deadlines. In that environment, it is almost impossible to have the right perspective to do strategic planning. Therefore, taking a break from that routine in an offsite session will almost always involve group brainstorming sessions covering one or more corporate issues. Correctly executed, these sessions can suggest new ideas that would have never surfaced during normal business.

These sessions can also have great team-building benefits for the staff. When folks work outside their regular job roles, they tend to drop the defensive barriers that dictate their daily habits. A few days without these barriers can help build relationships that can even continue when everyone is back on the job.

Be aware, however, that you can overdo things when you return to the everyday realities with your new inspirations. I once had a boss, who those of us reporting to him, learned to dread the times when he returned from a business trip. He would invariably return having read a magazine article on the airplane and insist on making major changes to how we were doing things. His staff would refer to his management style as "management by the latest *Business Week* article." We began conspiring to ensure he had a stack of reports to read on the airplane to prevent this problem.

Nevertheless, I am certain that some of his inspirations were beneficial. Many of the retreats and seminars that I participated in resulted in team bonding and fresh ideas for improving our business. There is something about being in a non-work environment that can be the catalyst for new ideas.

A Break for You (After reading this far, you need a break yourself.)

Yesterday, I had one of those minor medical procedures where they put you to sleep. As you are waking up from the anesthesia, the nurse comes into the room and runs through a long list of things that you cannot do for the next 24 hours. Of course, you never remember any of them as your head is still in a total fog. However, my wife says when the rather senior nurse finished reading the list, I asked her a question: "How about sex?" She replied that I would have to wait until tomorrow. I then asked her: "Should I come back to the hospital for that, or would she be able to come by the house?" I didn't remember saying that, but I sure remembered the kick from my wife. I thought I had made a good joke, but the nurse bested me when, after a pause, she said "Where do you live?"

Ok, now back to work...

Be a transparent Manager.

Classic management training at large companies teaches managers to embrace company decisions and directions blindly. The theme is that "subordinates must always view their manager as the voice of the company." An ambitious manager whose eye is on the top job will always follow that advice, even if he may disagree personally with the directive. Showing total devotion to the company is a requirement for staying in favor with higher management.

I remember walking into an unfamiliar area of the company and noticed several "Old Joe" types discussing a policy change in the company. As I waited to interrupt with a question, I overheard one of the Old Joes make the statement: "Of course, you can't believe what "he" says. He's a manager." That employee had obviously determined that what managers say, cannot be trusted. As a manager at the time, I wanted to respond. Punching him in the nose would have been temporarily satisfying, but the likely consequences forced my restraint. Instead, I simply asked my question and left.

After walking out, I began to reflect on the event. Every manager needs the complete trust and cooperation of their employees. That trust can be earned only if you are honest with your employees. That means, to be a manager trusted by your staff; you will have to occasionally ignore the corporate training of blindly following every direction and policy. Results are always better if you are simply honest with your employees.

Employees are more likely to embrace changes if they are fully informed. If you are being asked by higher management to implement a negative change for employees or an illogical work direction, don't try to make it sound logical or wise. Instead, simply explain the directive and why it is being given. Employees will respect you for it. An announcement from you, along the lines of "How can we best handle this new change?" will result in better support from the group. It will also keep employees talking to you instead of behind your back.

Similarly, I have never regretted revealing to my employees everything I knew about a company subject. If it is a change, let them know the reasons behind it and why alternatives were rejected. Of course, there are times when that course is inappropriate, such as discussing confidential information. But by and large, it is best to be as open as possible. If you can follow that practice, you will find that your authority comes from trust and respect instead of fear or assigned power. Trusted leadership builds teams that are motivated to help you succeed.

Resist One-hour Meetings

Executives tend to have their calendars filled up each day with one-hour meetings. There can be much wasted time in that hour.

A chief executive where I worked had an assistant who typically filled his daily schedule with one-hour meetings. I noticed something in those meetings. The CEO sat quietly and listened for 50 minutes. Then with 10 minutes left, he began asking several questions and gave his direction to their proposals or plans. I could not help but conclude that the meeting could have been 15 minutes long instead of an hour. Instead, the CEO did not engage until we were about to run out of time.

A manager I knew felt meetings were wasting too much time and took all the chairs and tables out of his conference room. He called them "stand-up" meetings. His theory was that if no one were comfortable, they would rush things along. It worked for a while, but soon people started coming into his conference room and sitting on the floor. And with that, meetings returned to historic lengths.

You have to set time limits for meetings. However, meetings don't have to take up all the scheduled time. When you have reached a conclusion, stop the meeting. The best solution is to determine ahead of time how long it should take to cover the subject and then set the time for the meeting. Fifteen-minute meetings can work. They can also provide the flexibility to schedule more time between meetings if you need to run over.

A technique that worked for me was to start the meeting by asking the purpose of the meeting and what we would like to accomplish. So many times, those two questions are obvious, as so many meetings are informational or working sessions, but there were occasions when those questions resulted in a postponed meeting. Answering them always set a tone for the meeting and resulted in shorter meetings.

Manage Your Ego

Having confidence in your own self-worth can have a calming influence when faced with uncomfortable circumstances such as important presentations. But, on the other hand, letting that self-worth go to your head can ruin your career.

I enjoy reading books about history. However, I have noticed that in most of these books, whether it was about Henry Ford, Lee Iacocca, Douglas MacArthur, or whoever, their weakness became their ego. As I looked at the monumental mistakes they made later in their career, I noticed that it was simply their ego that kept them from changing a position or making the right choice.

Once, when I became aware of a change that was about to be made in strategy by my company, I wrote a long e-mail to a friend whose job title was "Director of Strategy." I received a nice reply saying what a thorough and thoughtful analysis I had done. Then, that director called me and said that I didn't understand how things worked. He said that the boss (the President) tells us what we are going to do, and we do it. "Doing it" was how he kept his nice job. I didn't send him any more notes because I had a nice job too.

Not questioning the boss is always the best strategy for maintaining your job. However, if you are the boss who has fostered an unquestioning environment, you will be making big mistakes, and big mistakes can get you replaced. This means that when you are that boss, you are probably not being questioned. From experience, I can tell you that it is really nice not to be questioned. Unfortunately, you can also develop a god complex in that environment. It was what ruined so many of the famous people. Those history books are full of wars that were fought because egos prevented negotiation. Companies have suffered from the same phenomenon.

The lesson is to recognize this phenomenon and not lose the perspective that brought you to where you are today. For example, I mentioned earlier about developing a few trusted friends. They can be the sounding board. Soliciting opinions from your staff and encouraging discussion on critical issues can be a valuable grounding exercise. Exert your authority but listen to the opposition. Decisions made with the input of many are always better than edicts from the one. Not listening was undoubtedly one of the reasons Donald Trump was a one-term president. (I know, there were many reasons.)

8. BECOME A
MANAGEMENT PROFESSIONAL

When you Change Jobs, Do Nothing.

If you are starting at an entry level, ignore this tip. However, if you are the new manager, especially if it is a senior position, do nothing right away.

An executive I knew at IBM must have felt that he needed a total change of culture because he replaced his entire key staff with new people from outside the company. He hired six senior managers at the same time for critical positions in the company. An interesting thing happened fairly quickly.

First, almost all of the new managers started making pretty drastic changes in their operations. They made changes in staff, procedures, and general directions everywhere. I noticed these changes happening in every area except one. It seemed that this one new senior manager was doing almost nothing. As I watched him more closely, I eventually noticed that he was actually doing something. He was listening to his staff and learning the business. It was a year before he started doing anything that I would consider innovative, and that was simply something that his staff had wanted to do for a long time.

A funny thing happened to that brand-new senior staff. Within 18 months of their hiring, only one of the six was still an employee of the company. The lone survivor (you have already guessed who he was) later became a senior executive in the company.

The lesson is this: When you are hired as a fresh manager in a new area, you are going to feel obligated to make quick changes to impress higher management. You will certainly be given lots of suggestions tempting you to show that you are making a difference. Resist that temptation. Do nothing but listen for six months. It will pay off in the end.

Occasionally, Create a Crisis

People work best during a crisis. When things become too calm, try creating a crisis. When work is stagnant, people seem to find issues to argue and bicker about.

In a crisis, everyone pulls together and ignores the little problems that cause arguments. **Work also tends to expand to fill the time allotted.** In a crisis, workers are always more efficient. Often, innovators and heroes are born.

One of my best friends related an exciting time at IBM when he participated in a big crisis. They were building the unit that would control the first-stage rocket boosters to put a man on the moon. It seems that, as a former track star, he had been chosen to stand for several hours next to a master toolmaker who was using a one-of-a-kind machine to produce a small and extremely complicated part. When the toolmaker finished, he turned around and dropped the part in a small, foam-lined box that my friend held.

My friend shut the box and took off, running through one building and then another until reaching the main lobby. Two police cars were waiting at the front door. As he dove into the back seat of the second car, they took off with lights and sirens going full blast. When they reached the airport, they drove right out onto the runway to a waiting Air Force fighter jet. My friend jumped out of the car, ran up the portable boarding ladder, and dropped the box into the lap of the officer in the second seat. The jet was in the air and gone before he got back to the police car.

That crisis was a deadline. Deadlines can be the incentive to force a crisis, but so can technical problems or sales goals. A crisis will build a team, and teams are always more productive. A good manager will occasionally reap surprising benefits in his organization by creating a crisis. All it has to be is a goal, with a deadline. Those deadlines always exist. Making it a crisis will strengthen and unify your team.

I created something of a crisis once without knowing it. Our production standard for each assembly line stated that every assembly line should produce 800 products per shift. We were currently averaging a little over 700 per assembly line. What I did was to announce that the assembly line that built the most products during the week would have free pizza on Friday. A funny thing happened. By the end of the day Friday, every one of the nine assembly lines had averaged over 800 per day, with the winning line producing just over 1,000 units.

This plant was in Mexico where it was customary to provide free breakfast and lunch every day. I suppose pizza was special. Another aspect the managers pointed out to me was that peer pressure on the lines had become the real motivator. If one employee was not pulling his load, his peers immediately confronted him.

One possible factor of this phenomenon was the famous "Hawthorne effect," which is that the simple act of showing management interest could have a positive effect. Another contributor undoubtedly was the influence of competition between the numerous assembly lines. However, the biggest lesson for me was to see the apparent benefit of rewarding the team rather than the individual. In many ways, the role of the supervisor was replaced by peer members of the team.

I wanted to take that lesson and create a permanent system of reward for team performance. I was hoping that we might be able to adopt an incentive system that would provide a cash bonus for meeting and exceeding the daily standard. However, I never figured out how to make it sustainable. I had noticed similar programs become entitlements rather than incentives. So instead, we just kept giving out pizza.

Deadlines, cost goals, and production goals are always reasonable, tangible targets that teams can rally around. But, often, the rally is the real benefit rather than the target.

Adopt a "Program Du Jour"

Another team-building technique is to adopt one of the classic programs for improving processes. Dozens are available, like Lean Manufacturing, Six Sigma, ISO Certifications, etc. There is usually one in fashion at the moment that will sound appealing, always with the promise of revolutionary improvements.

Anytime a new program is adopted, it will result in real, measurable improvements. The improvements might be another example of the "Hawthorne effect" of management showing interest, or it might be because of tangible improvements to current procedures.

In addition, if the program involves any of the recognized certifications (i.e., ISO 9000 or 6 Sigma for quality, R2 or LEED for Environmental, etc.), there is an added benefit for marketing. Often, large corporations require one of these certifications for all their suppliers. I was surprised to see how many large companies would forgo a qualification survey of the company I was working for if we were ISO- and R2-certified.

However, be careful not to let the "program" become the product. Companies occasionally begin to focus on the complicated regulations or program requirements and forget that they are trying to make a profit. I have seen this happen repeatedly. The company dedicates entire departments to training, implementing, and policing this grand new program. That's where you have to be careful.

To minimize the opportunity for the program becoming the product, implement the new program, reap the short-term benefit, and then let it die. Sometimes that is difficult because you get particularly good at policing and creating more and more bureaucracy for the company. Figuring out that tipping point will be difficult. However, not doing so could affect the bottom line. One option is to start looking at another program. There will always be another.

A book on this subject is Tim Hindle's *Guide to Management Ideas and Gurus*. It includes lists of programs along with a description of benefits.

Budget High

Always budget enough money and headcount to get the job done. Unfortunately, in some companies, this may require some creative forethought.

Large corporations must plan ahead to ensure financial stability and adequate funds for daily operations. The Studebaker Automotive Company is often cited as an example of a company that failed because of the lack of adequate cost planning, resulting in their underpricing of their cars. This planning is usually performed on an annual basis with every department required to submit a budget for the following year. As all the budgets are rolled together, the company can predict financial results for the next year. Unfortunately, these results often do not meet expectations. That means that budgets must be cut to achieve the results. The cut often means that managers will have to resubmit a new budget, frequently including a specific percent reduction.

Managers who exceed their budgets have great difficulty thriving in a corporate environment. One way to avoid that difficulty is to intentionally exaggerate or buffer your initial submission of an annual budget. A friend of mine made the mistake of trying for humor when he asked a question in a management kickoff of the annual planning cycle. He had been through many of these budget exercises and simply asked if they had any idea how large the cuts were going to be this year. I am sure his budget attracted more scrutiny that year.

One easy way to buffer a budget is by exaggerating the size of staff required to achieve the work. It is difficult for executive management to make accurate assessments of staffing requirements. As a result, it is not unusual to see areas grossly over-or understaffed in the same company. That weakness provides an opportunity for a buffer in your budget. This weakness will allow you to make the required cuts without jeopardizing your ability to accomplish your objectives. And, if there are no cuts, it will make you a hero next year for finishing under budget.

If you do end up with a buffered final budget, resist the temptation to overstaff. It is difficult to manage an overstaffed area. Overstaffed areas tend to foster poor employee relationships, bickering, and problems. You will spend too much time settling disputes and creating meaningful workloads. Managing an understaffed area is actually much easier. Everyone is too busy to get mixed up in petty arguments.

Note: If you are the senior executive, controller, or financial manager in a major company, you need to give serious consideration to this tip. If everyone follows this guide, then the corporate budgets are worthless. The way to avoid that outcome when cuts are necessary is to take a different approach. Cutting budgets by a percentage may work once, but soon managers will simply begin to anticipate and buffer their submission. Instead, cut expenses, programs, or plans. Reducing employment tends to be one of the early considerations. For that option, be aware that the essence of the company comes from what its people can do. Losing them reduces the value of the company.

Develop and Protect your Suppliers

Corporations often become heavily dependent upon a few key suppliers. How these relationships are managed can be a vital success factor for a company.

Early in my career, I was working on a major expansion of a plastics facility and was responsible for purchasing the large industrial equipment that produced plastic products. The selected supplier was able to quickly provide the equipment as he had accurately predicted our need and preordered the expensive machinery. That supplier was a single-owner small distributor run by a very competent businessman. His planning had significantly helped in getting our factory up and going in record time.

A couple of months after the equipment delivery, the owner contacted me with a request. It seemed that my company had not paid his invoices, which was putting a real strain on his operating cash. When I contacted our accounting department about the payment, I was told that our company was not paying any bills until next year. The supplier was not going to get paid for five months. They told me not to give this information to the supplier but rather simply tell him that there was a paperwork problem, and he would receive payment soon. That is exactly what I did.

The memory and personal regret associated with my acquiescing to the company position during that period caused a change in me. I vowed to try to deal upfront and fairly with everyone, including suppliers. I know my company caused a hardship for this supplier, and I was disrespectful and unprofessional in the way I handled it. After that experience, I tried to be honest and transparent with suppliers and learned later that there would be times when it genuinely paid off.

Many years later, I remember calling a key supplier late one afternoon with an urgent request. It seemed that we had a major product failure and needed that supplier to make a quick run of a critical part to replace our problematic products. It was an emergency because we had to have the parts before the 7:00 AM start of the first shift the next morning. The supplier said that the tooling that produced that part was defective, but he would see what he could do.

The next morning, I walked into the plant around 6:30 and was greeted by one of the supervisors, who said, "The truck is here!" I followed him back to the loading dock and was in time to see that supplier's 18-wheel truck backing up to the dock. Then, as one of our dock workers opened the trailer doors, I witnessed something incredible. There were six people with tools in hand, reworking defective parts in the back of that truck. During the night-long journey from the supplier's factory, they had reworked enough parts to allow us to start production. They had produced the only parts they could with the defective tooling and then had reworked them during the night as the truck made the four-hour trip to our factory. We obviously had a good working relationship with that supplier.

Treating suppliers fairly and maintaining an honest relationship will yield the type of support that keeps your company successful. But don't forget, there is a delicate balance that must be maintained to prevent any possibility of collusion or impropriety. Therefore, the relationship must always follow the "arm's-length principle."

The best way to maintain an arms-length relationship and still benefit from the partnership is to understand the supplier's business fully. This understanding must neither include interference nor can it imply a quid pro quo relationship. Visit their operations. Understand their processes and their dependencies. When you have done that, you are also in a much better position to negotiate pricing and to leverage their technology and capabilities.

Maintain your Own In-House Experts

While it is true that the expertise at suppliers can be leveraged, it is always best to have your own experts. Or, as my old boss used to say, **"Experience is nontransferable."** That tacit knowledge is extremely valuable to an organization. Unfortunately, it often includes trade secrets and techniques that are not documented.

One day, I was in my office having a discussion with old "Harry Ears" (remember Old Joe?) when one of the new engineers stopped by to give me an update. He had been working on an urgent change to a part at one of our suppliers that would solve a problem with one of our products. I had asked him to let me know when he received a response from the vendor. The new engineer reported that it would take the supplier a week to make the necessary changes to the tooling. That would put us behind in our production schedule.

Old "Hairy Ears" overheard the conversation and said only one thing: "Hand me that telephone." I scooted the phone over the side of the desk and watched him start dialing. In about 30 seconds, he had the owner of that supplier on the phone. The words he used in the conversation were not something I would want to repeat here, but the gist was that he was offering to show the owner how to operate the equipment in his own plant. He told that owner exactly how long it would take him to make our change and when he expected it to be complete (eight hours from that moment).

The young engineer learned something from that exercise while it simply reminded me of the importance of maintaining your own experts. Most of these experts learned their specialty by doing it themselves, which presents a particular problem for companies that outsource more and more of their activities. Keeping your experts up to date becomes difficult, as they might not be current with new techniques that have developed since their personal involvement. As a result, the jobs of the experts must be expanded to include keeping up with technological advances.

Developing replacements for experts can also be challenging. They are usually older and tend to retire early. I am not certain why, but I have also noted that they are often the type of strongly opinioned employee who is more likely to be fired.

And if your company has chosen to outsource the fundamental technologies of its business, it will be impossible to train experts internally. The required skills will need to be recruited from the outside or created by investing in formal training of your current staff. The training will involve much travel, as well as frequently expensive classes and seminars. Whichever way you use to develop the internal expertise, you will find them invaluable.

Try to Consider the "why" Behind the Statement

A common business idiom refers to the benefit of having a 30,000-foot view of a problem, which is good advice for managers. It can relate to remembering to include the big picture in any discussion. It can also relate to remembering to consider why someone might have a particular view or opinion. Understanding why someone is taking a specific stand on an issue can be immensely helpful in resolving conflicts and establishing common ground.

A manager who reported to me came into my office one day saying that a new employee had just taken credit for something that he, the manager, had been working on personally for a long time. He was upset because he had done all the work and therefore should have been the one to get credit for the work. Instead of jumping into the blame game with him, I asked him why the new employee might have done that. As we talked it through, he was able to conclude that the new employee was feeling very insecure in his job and must have been looking for acceptance. Instead of wishing he could punch the guy in the nose, he left thinking of ways to help that employee feel more confident in his job. He had found the root cause of the problem. Fixing the root cause is always better than simply reacting to an emotion.

Procrastination can also be your friend at times of apparent, big problems. Pausing provides time to analyze the cause of the problem instead of implementing a quick fix. Procrastination was always easy for me. What surprised me was that sometimes the problem solved itself while I deliberated.

Taking the time to think beyond your first thought before responding or commenting is especially important in meetings. Ask yourself, "What effect will what I am about to say have?" Sometimes, you think of something to say that is relevant and noteworthy, but it might not serve a useful purpose to say it. Instead, it might make someone else look bad or wrong in their position. As a result, you could end up creating an adversary without knowing it.

Be a "Show Me" and "Why" Manager.

A good technique for fixing the root cause is not forgetting to say, "Show me." It is always tempting to take immediate action when a subordinate reports a problem that could have negative consequences. A much more effective approach is to ask questions and understand the detail before acting. Stories often seem to have a way of changing when you understand the detail and do the analysis yourself.

I was hired as a consultant at a large company to function as a temporary manager while the usual executive completed a three-month training program in Europe. During the overview/orientation on the first day, the senior executive mentioned that I would be seeing a purchase order soon for a $3 million upgrade in the factory utilities infrastructure.

Two weeks later the purchase order appeared on my desk for approval. The more I looked at it, the more questions I had about why this work was needed. Finally, I asked the manager in the area involved to "show me" the data behind the request. As he began showing me the reasons for the change, it became obvious that a supplier, who needed work, had recommended the changes. I requested that our engineers review the data and conduct an internal analysis. Two weeks later, that analysis concluded that the problem could be fixed by using only 10% of the expected funds. By putting more effort into the analysis, we could avoid spending most of the $3 million.

Occasionally completing the analysis yourself is also an excellent way to achieve the tone with your employees that will keep poorly thought out issues from getting to your office. If employees know that you will ask for the details, they will do a much better analysis.

Management by Walking Around is a term coined by Tom Peters in the book *In Search of Excellence.* It suggests the same theme of talking to others personally and asking questions. However, you will have to be careful to ensure that making that technique your management style does not undermine your own staff. Always use the information to discuss with your staff instead of directing specific actions. Nevertheless, seeing the operation regularly, as well as being seen, can be a valuable practice. It will help you learn things that might not be getting to your office, and it will show management interest in the operations.

To summarize, don't forget to ask employees **"why"** and **"Show me."** And don't forget to ask yourself why someone might be saying what you are hearing. Knowing where someone is coming from can help identify the best solution to a problem.

Never Make Offhand Comments.

The toughest thing about facing death isn't the experiences you won't get to have. It's the ones you can't have back. Similarly, managers can often be embarrassed to discover that employees have repeated and often misconstrued and offhand comment.

Before we got married, my young wife-to-be and I visited her grandmother. As soon as we walked into her house, she looked up and said, "You don't look too fat in that dress." (Emphasizing the "that dress."). If my wife's grandmother were around today, she would be embarrassed to see me using that example. The same embarrassment can happen to a manager who makes an offhand comment without thinking.

A manager's words receive far more scrutiny than the average employee. It is similar to politicians and political candidates. It is easy to find examples of where a politician suffered greatly from an offhand comment that may have been intended as sarcasm or humor. Similarly, managers can find themselves suffering because of an offhand or idle comment. A good practice for avoiding this circumstance is to give serious thought to every single thing you say. Remember to ask yourself how what you are saying might be misconstrued or be offensive to someone else. As I learned that lesson (the hard way), I often found myself laughing, or at least grinning, in a meeting at something I was thinking to say, but didn't.

Provide an Effective Office Environment

Having the right office environment can significantly improve professional productivity.

I have worked from home, in a large building with a virtual sea of adjacent desks, in shared office space with six others, in individual cubicles, in two-person shared offices and in an individual office. Some of these configurations were dictated by facility availability, some by philosophy, and some by paranoid senior management, who felt like they needed to see all the heads down.

A senior VP at one of my first companies, which had the "sea of desks" would occasionally walk down the center isle and take names of the heads that were not down. The people on his "list" seemed to disappear from the office the next day. One of the supervisors I knew sat close to the VP's office complex and would reflexively pick up the phone and pretend to be talking whenever he saw a shadow. He ended up having a nervous breakdown.

When I worked in the "sea of desks" it was difficult to concentrate on work. Inevitably, someone would turn around and say to someone near, "did you see that game last night?" Of course, several others who had seen the game had heard the question and immediately entered the conversation. Those, non-work-related conversations happened all day long.

I had the same problem when I shared an office with a team member. It was impossible not to overhear a phone conversation and have questions or try to help out by offering suggestions. And you would feel discourteous if you didn't ask about family situations or other non-work-related subjects first thing in the morning. I remember feeling twice as productive when I finally had my own office.

Of course, individual cubicles can offer similar privacy for maximizing personal productivity. Working from home can be equally productive if you can keep from being distracted by everything in that environment. A dedicated home office area is essential, which may be impossible for some employees. The problem I had with working from home is that I could never leave work. I found that when I had an idea in the shower, instead of writing it down to consider for tomorrow, I went in and started working on it, no matter what time it was. Sometimes those sessions could last most of the night. My company might have appreciated the extra effort, but my wife certainly didn't.

There are other office environmental nuances that can enhance productivity. Having an in-house cafeteria, free coffee, close break areas, white noise generators for open areas, nearby conference rooms, good lighting, comfortable temperatures, can all improve office efficiency. If you have the luxury of building new, consider hiring a professional. I was able to do that once and was impressed by their insights and suggestions. Also, invest in ergonomic furniture. A back problem motivated me to pay $1300 for an office chair that I could not part with today. It looks a little funny because the back is wide at the top and narrow at the waist. I noticed right away that I could comfortably have my arms by my side because the back of the chair didn't interfere.

To summarize, spend time on this subject, analyze your constraints, and consider options for improving daily efficiency. The investment can have an impressive payback.

9. Make Your Style a Differentiator

Pick Up Trash – The world is changed by your example, not by your opinion. (Paul Coelho)

When you are walking through your operation, pick up the trash. Your actions have a more significant impact than your words.

When Bill Clinton was president and campaigning for NAFTA, he toured the plant where I worked. He was using our modern factory as an example for successful U.S. manufacturing. My production lines were the focus of the tour. In preparation, I gave a thorough tour to the president of our company. As I was taking him through the assembly area the first time, he surprised me twice by bending down to pick up a small piece of trash.

Of course, I was a little embarrassed that trash was present for him to pick up. The point, though, was that everyone on that assembly line noticed what the company president did. Of course, we had cleaning people to pick up trash, but the president demonstrated that no one was above the job of taking responsibility for his workplace. Our company president's action made a point, and the point was not lost on any of us. **Quality work is done in a quality place**.

Sometimes actions of a manager can speak louder than words. It is not just picking up the trash. It is all the small things that you do yourself to set an example for how you expect others to act. As a manager, you are always being observed by others. So, setting the example yourself can be a powerful tool in setting the tone for your area.

As an aside, that presidential visit was certainly a memorable experience. Having secret service people follow you around for a week is kind of neat. Bill (we are on a first-name basis now) used my office while he was there and actually remembered my name when talking to someone else. Also, many of our employees were not allowed to come to work that day because of issues with their security checks. (No one lost any pay. It was a bonus vacation day for them.)

The day of the event I went home all pumped up because everything had gone so well. That was until I came into the house. I had gone into the kitchen and turned on a little TV while I got something out of the refrigerator. I glanced at the TV and right there on CNN I was standing next to the president while he gave a talk on NAFTA. I ran into the living room where my daughter and wife were watching TV and said: "Change the channel, I'm on national TV!" My daughter looked at me and said: "Dad, we see you all the time. This is a good show." I went back to the kitchen to watch myself. Sometimes, it takes a little girl to remind you that your ego is getting a little out of hand.

As a second aside, soon after NAFTA was passed, we moved that manufacturing to Mexico. (Remember the four reasons for moving manufacturing?)

Keep your Feet on the Ground.

Managers are treated with greater deference by everyone as they move up the ladder. If a manager is not careful, he will start believing he really is special.

When I started working at IBM, I received six promotions in less than three years. I had gone from being a starting engineer to being a third-level manager. I was certainly making good career progress. It doesn't take long in this environment before you begin to feel that you really are special. The things I said always seemed to be profound. After all, no one ever argued with me. It was about the time that my wife and I started having problems. She obviously did not understand how special I was.

Everything at work, however, was going great for me. After all, I had become the grand panjandrum. Then, one day I arrived at work to find a single-page article in the middle of my beautiful mahogany desk. It was all about bosses becoming gods in their own minds. That was a clear wake-up call for me. I had taken pride in thinking that I was a sensitive people person. But, instead, I had become a real jerk.

A management practice that I was using occasionally reminded me of how "not special" I am. As I mentioned before, the method was to regularly conduct one-on-one interviews with people at every level in my organization. When I first started implementing this, I was amazed at how intelligent and capable every hourly assembly line worker was. Almost all of them were intelligent people who simply missed an opportunity somewhere along their paths. Many of the folks I spent time with had ideas for improvements, much better than mine.

Later in my career, that awareness helped me become a successful consultant. Most consultants would tour customer facilities to analyze processes for the purpose of finding ways for improving the company. Not me. Instead, I would ask to have one-on-one interviews with key people and folks on the assembly lines and process areas. I then simply asked the employee what they would like to change to make improvements and offered to put their ideas in front of the top management. Invariably, one of the employees would pull out a sketch or share a vision of a totally different approach to one of their company's processes. I would then put that idea into a presentable form and take it to management. Management was often amazed at my insight and usually hired me for an extended engagement. (Yes, I did give credit to the employee … eventually.)

To summarize, as a manager, you are going to be treated as if you are special. You are not special. Don't forget that.

Sometimes you Will Need to be Simply "A Lot of People"

A good manager will always be sensitive to the personal lives of employees. A sagacious man once said to me, "**You only get one chance to go to a wedding or a funeral.**" Going to a wedding or funeral is an excellent way to show that you care. People always remember that you were there and appreciate that.

I have never forgotten the feeling I had when I stood up to do a eulogy at my mother's funeral and saw my boss and an employee sitting in the audience. They had driven five hours to be there. I had an excellent boss at that time.

Of course, sometimes, you will get the impression that you are simply adding to the crowd. However, those will be the times that you are adding tremendous value for the employee. When that new bride or bereaved spouse turns around at that wedding or funeral, they need to see a lot of people. Being simply "a lot of people" can be of enormous emotional value to someone. An outstanding manager will be one of "a lot of people" often.

10. SECURING THE TOP

Note: It bears repeating at this point that to make it to the top of a company, you have to be qualified and do a good job. You also have to be a capable manager. This section, along with the example in the Preface, identifies practices that those who succeed in achieving the coveted top position, always seem to follow.

Keep your Personal Interest First.

If your goal is reaching the top of the corporation, your personal interest must always be paramount in all your actions, especially your positions on issues. Sometimes you may feel that the wise position to take is not the best position for the company. Managers who advance up the corporate ladder most smoothly always make "the wise" decision.

While serving as a midlevel engineering manager in a fortune 500 company, my team was assigned to contribute to a new program that the top manager had proposed. After a few months of dedicated effort, our team had concluded that this program was not a good fit for the company. The most significant problem was that it simply did not make any financial sense. We could not build a competitive product using that technology.

As the financial function in that company had a separate reporting structure, I felt obligated to review our data with the financial organization. Our area's finance manager agreed to look into the program and conduct his own analysis. After a couple of weeks, he met with me and shared his results that indicated that the business analysis was even worse than our initial assessment. I suggested that he be the one to take this information to top management, as it was a financial problem. He agreed and said that he would set up the appropriate meetings.

As time passed, I noticed that he had not taken the bad news forward. Several times I stopped by his office to ask what the holdup was. Every time, he seemed to sidestep the subject by saying there had been a delay in setting up the meetings. Eventually, I gave up asking. My group had transferred the program to another area in the company, and I had other things to worry about. However, as time passed, I learned that the negative information was never presented, and the program wasted millions of dollars, just as our original analysis predicted.

Why didn't the financial manager take the information forward? The answer is simple. The CEO of the company had personally suggested this new program and pushed it along with frequent requests for status updates. Presenting negative information to that CEO would obviously reflect poorly on his decisions. Furthermore, it is human nature not to like anyone who makes them look bad (kill the messenger syndrome). Therefore, the astute financial manager chose not to be the one who made the CEO look bad. That was the wise decision for him to make, although it put his personal interests above the interests of the company. The company eventually wasted millions on that program, but that astute manager's career continued to flourish. In fact, he ultimately became president of the company.

At another time, working in that same role, my boss had concluded that the new product development program we were working on was in danger of missing its completion schedule. This delay would be costly for the company, as it would involve additional engineering investment and change marketing strategies. A peer middle manager and I helped our boss put together a presentation for the purpose of informing top management of the problem. Our boss invited the two of us to accompany him for the session where he would be presenting the appropriate top executive with the bad news.

When the time for the meeting came, the peer and I walked together to the exec's office. As we sat down, we learned from the secretary that the exec and our boss were in another meeting and would be a little late. After she left, I turned to the peer and said: "You know, if we were astute, we would not be here. This is a bad-news meeting, and the exec is going to associate us with the bad news." The peer looked at me, got up, and left. I stayed because I felt obligated to support my boss. That peer manager was obviously astute. Eight years later, he rose to the level of general manager of the entire site. He was a capable and astute manager. Astute managers, who put their own career first in their actions, tend to advance in an organization, which occasionally makes them also be a jerk.

I enjoyed knowing a cantankerous senior manufacturing manager at IBM. His strong British accent and loud voice always dominated meetings and commanded respect. When IBM decided to meet the Japanese computer competition by automating its factories, he was asked to head up a significant effort for automating our main product. After spending time analyzing the plan, he decided it was unrealistic and impractical.

When top management found that he was not supporting the program, they found another person to take the job. The British manager was moved to a support role and eventually retired from the company. However, the person who took the job flourished in the company, as he oversaw the spending of 650 million dollars on automation.

As you might have guessed, shortly after the automation was implemented, the decision was made to abandon the effort. The complicated automation did not function as hoped. The automation took months to adjust and reprogram, which threatened to delay the introduction of new products. The cost of the enormous engineering effort to keep the automated factory running also far exceeded the anticipated labor savings. The automation was ultimately bulldozed out of the factory. It didn't work. It was a bad idea and, as the British manager had pointed out, impractical.

The British manager had tried to do the right thing for the company but lost personally. The financial manager did the wrong thing for the company but gained personally. The lesson and the best practice to follow for getting ahead is: Always do what is best for you personally. That action, however, can sometimes make you feel like a jerk.

Sailing Can be Rewarding.

Before you take a position on a subject that could be controversial, find out which way the wind is blowing.

A highly successful executive I worked for once would often frustrate me when I brought up a new subject. He would listen without commenting positively or negatively but say that he would get back to me later. I had observed that this senior executive seemed to be singularly focused on identifying what position the president of the company might have before taking a position on anything. In fact, he spent a great deal of his time trying to covertly determine what that position might be through assistants and secretaries.

When he satisfied himself with what the president would favor, he immediately established a solid position supporting that view. He often then took an argument for that view to the president for approval. This became an advantageous career tactic for that manager. The lesson for the astute manager is to find out which way the wind is blowing on an issue, **put up your sail and let the wind take you up the ladder.**

* *   * *   * *

So, you've decided to do the "right thing"? When you decide to do the "right thing" by speaking up against the way the wind is blowing, you need to remember something. You rarely receive the later opportunity to say: "I told you so." You rarely receive credit for changing directions or achieving a goal when you have bucked the system. Search inside yourself instead, for comfort in knowing you didn't have to say later: "I wish I had said something." Being able to know that you did the right thing, can be very satisfying. (However, you will miss out on getting one of my "jerk" badges.)

Never Go Around your Boss.

Go around your boss only as an absolute last resort. (Like when the building is on fire, or the business is about to go under.)

Once I found myself working for one of my good friends. He was new in the position and seemed to be suffering from a lack of confidence in picking the best choice for the various options for the design of our new products. Every time a major study was completed showing the features and possibilities of different future products, he would request another study, usually with expensive consultants.

As a result, we wasted money and lost precious development time required to compete in the market.

We managers who reported to this new executive became increasingly frustrated with the indecision and began to have meetings among ourselves to discuss ideas for dealing with the situation. As the one who best knew this executive, I was elected to meet with the company's senior executive to ask for his help. I agreed and put together a presentation that delineated the problem and the action we recommended for the senior executive. We recommended that the senior executive look over our boss's shoulder to help him make this one crucial decision. A little support from him would have been what our boss needed to return to his field of expertise, managing a program.

The senior executive's reaction surprised me. He agreed with our observations but had a totally different conclusion for action. He fired our boss. What a mistake I had made. I had lost a friend, a sponsor, and the company had lost a great manager. In addition, the senior executive probably concluded that he should not trust me to be loyal. I had forgotten to consider that senior executives are almost always jerks and forgotten to consider how my action might affect my personal career. My mistake was going around my boss. Instead, I should have kept my mouth shut.

Sometimes it is tough going to your boss with an issue where you are sure he is making a mistake. However, taking the issue to him will always be a better option than going around him. Make your case to him, privately and delicately, because this is the person who has the most control of your destiny. Prepare well, present the facts, but don't argue. In my example, we had tried that, but failed. I wish I had tried again.

I had another boss once who would vehemently argue his position until I conceded his point. Then, a few days later, I would often witness him changing his position to match my argument when the subject came up with others. At first, I concluded that he had to think about these things overnight. But then later, I realized that he simply could not lose an argument or admit to being wrong. Whatever the reason, delicately presenting a differing point ultimately had the desired effect. He did change his position.

Make your Own Presentations

Every step along the path to the top of a company will depend upon the impression you are making with higher management. One way to ensure you are getting positive visibility with higher management is always to be the person making the presentations to them.

Several times in my early career, I became agitated when the work that I had finished was presented to upper management by my boss. Why didn't he let me make the presentation? It was my work. What I didn't understand at the time was that his management expected him to know the information. It was also a way for him to take credit for the work and advance his own status. I could not help but feel that my boss was being a jerk when he did these things.

On the other hand, as a manager, I always tried to have the person most familiar with the work make the presentation. The reason was a combination of my stage fright and my desire to have the person with the most information doing the talking. I now realize that I was missing the opportunity to advance my standing, along with being a jerk to my employee.

Keep your Best People

The quality and capability of a manager's staff is the most important factor in determining whether a manager successfully executes his area's responsibilities. Finding and retaining competent people is the essential key to maintaining a capable staff. This was a difficult lesson for me to learn.

Senior management in big companies will frequently ask for lists of candidates for promotional opportunities. Early on, I would put my best performers on that list. However, I noticed something: Some of the most effective managers seemed to put mediocre employees from their groups on the list. I also noticed that it was the mediocre employees who were often selected for promotion. It finally dawned on me that the managers were selfishly protecting their best people. They simply didn't want to lose their highest performers.

Does that mean that a top performer might not get an opportunity for promotion? It can. As you will always be a top performer, make sure your management is aware of your career goals so that your name remains on the list for promotional consideration. Good managers are usually sympathetic to employee aspirations. It is also helpful to inform the next-higher level of management of your career goals.

On a personal note, as soon as I realized that successful managers were not putting their best people on the promotion lists, I remembered my successful start of employment at IBM, when I had received six promotions in three years. How deflating to realize that I must have been a profoundly mediocre employee.

I have known managers who said that they could build people into what they needed. That doesn't work. A better plan is to try to fit the job to the person, rather than the person to the job. Just like the best college coaches are the best recruiters, not the best game coaches. Michael Jordan types are born, not built. The best coaches find the gifted players and hold onto them. You will want to do the same.

Treat People as Numbers.

Reaching the top of a company requires success in the activities under your responsibility. Having and keeping good people is one key to that success. However, at the top of the company, responsibilities change. At the top of the company, a prime responsibility is to improve profits. (Also, a key factor determining compensation at the top of the company.)

All businesses have good times and bad times. During the bad times, the easiest way to maintain profits is by cutting employees. A logical way to do that is by ranking employees and laying off those with the lowest ranking. Another option for reducing employment is to conduct layoffs based on compensation. Eliminating high-cost employees first will yield a higher benefit in reducing expenses. However, the best option for layoffs is to rank employees by job category, focusing on the higher-paid classifications, which can eliminate higher-paid people who are also poor performers.

As the top manager, employees may view you as a jerk for implementing one of these programs. However, it is the best way to improve profits in slow times. One benefit often cited by executive management is the opportunity to ultimately improve labor quality. Laying off poor-performing employees during bad times opens the possibility of hiring higher-quality replacements during good times.

I have seen employment reduction used for maintaining or increasing short-term profits so many times that I know it should be high on the list of executive actions. However, when this happens, I have been worried that the company is nothing more than the people and what they can do. With every layoff, part of the company is lost.

Also, when the better managers in an organization are required to implement one of these reduction programs, it will be their worst day of employment. Telling someone that they no longer have any visible means of support is a difficult thing to have to do. I know one excellent manager who quit a very good job because he could not do it.

Implementing these programs also tends to change the environment in the workplace for employees. Employees will naturally feel more anxious and even threatened by the event. Cooperation in departments tends to be strained as everyone realizes that their performance is being compared to their peers in a more ominous way. Management should make future plans clear to employees to minimize this anxiety. An assurance that the current layoff will not be repeated for at least 12 months is one way to provide employees a bit of relief for the moment.

Of course, a senior manager can take actions to avoid being considered a jerk. Cutting costs or liquidating assets should be high on that list. There are also several options for reducing labor costs without laying off employees. Across-the-board pay cuts have worked exceptionally well with tech companies, which tend to have high-paid employees. Other options include reducing hours worked per week and offering extra days of unpaid vacation. The risk with these programs is that high-performing employees may leave the company. However, these more-compassionate programs are the best way to be positioned for an upturn in business while reducing the impact to employee morale.

Be Cautious about Being Honest with Employees.

Remember when I mentioned that I took a chance being honest with the young engineer and told him to spend money on a haircut and clothes? I was taking a chance because there was a potential negative consequence for me. What if he had made an issue of that with the human resources department? For the same reason, astute managers are rarely candid when appraising employees. There is always a risk to the manager when he confronts or documents negative behavior. The manager will be creating a disgruntled employee. And disgruntled employees can always find subtle ways to sabotage a manager's performance. Being honest and transparent with your employees will make you a better manager, but it can also jeopardize your opportunity to get to the top.

Nevertheless, there will be times when you are required to be honest with employees about a sensitive or personal area. For example, I had an employee who had an annoying body odor. I could tell if he was in his office if I simply started walking down the long aisle leading to his office. After other employees complained to me about this, I knew that I had to talk with this man. At first, I wanted to lightheartedly ask if he had been chewing on his socks again but realized that this had to be more serious. So, I brought up the subject by asking if he was on any medication that would cause an odor. That let me get into what I had noticed. It also resulted in him fixing the problem, even though personal hygiene was not a priority in his native culture. (And no, he was not one of my cousins from Tennessee.)

The astute manager with aspirations for the top will find it preferable to simply transfer a dysfunctional employee to another area of the company rather than address the problem. This shifts the problem to someone else and avoids having to take the more drastic measure of firing the employee. With the many U.S. labor law restrictions, firing an employee can be a very unpleasant task.

11. REFLECT ON THE CHOICES

Unfortunate Consequences for Managers

The plusses for making it to the top of a corporation are numerous: money, ego, self-fulfillment, etc. However, unanticipated side effects can be negative and disappointing. Some of them can even lead to regrets because **it is easy to lose your way in a career.**

I lost my way when I joined IBM. The contrast between their culture and the other three Fortune 500 companies where I had worked, was incredible. They practiced this "respect for the individual" in everything they did. Work became fun and I fell in love with it. And it surely loved me because I had reached the third level of management in my third year of employment.

I was reminded of losing my way one day when I was cleaning out the basement at our house (which meant shifting boxes around). As I picked up one of the boxes, a picture fell out on to the floor. When I picked it up, I noticed that it was a little snaggletooth girl of five or six. My wife was walking by at the time, and I held up the picture and asked which one of our daughter's friends this was? She glanced at the picture and kept walking over to the other side of the basement. I thought she probably didn't see the picture and followed her over to the other side. After she stopped, I held it up again and repeated the question. She said, "You mean, you don't recognize your own daughter"?

I didn't say anything else. My wife went back upstairs. I kept looking at the picture and thinking: Let's see, six years old, that was probably the year that we first introduced our first revolutionary printer, or maybe it was the second, or maybe the third. Boy, that was a busy time! I didn't take any vacation that year. I can even remember working Christmas Day. My picture was on the cover of a couple of magazines that year. I guess that was actually a typical year. It was one of the years that I was reaching for every brass ring that came around.

Somewhere along the line, I stopped reaching for the brass rings. It was probably after I broke my finger a few times. Of course, by then my daughter was already in college. Someone asked me if I was able to regain the lost relationship with my daughter. Sadly, the answer is no. It is like asking, how well you made a first impression the second time. You only get one chance to make a first impression. If you blow it, it's gone.

I still have copies of the magazines with my picture on them. Someday, I will show them to my daughter. I wish I had a picture of me in a baseball cap with my hand on the shoulder of a snaggletooth girl instead.

The further you go up the corporate ladder, the more of your life the company owns. In aspiring to top management, you will be giving up much of your personal life. Your time is the only gift you can give your family that you can never get back. Executives often say that the little time they have to spend with their family is quality time. How do you designate time as "quality time"?

The wife of a top executive once related a story to me about her husband. She said that on the third day of their one-week annual vacation, her husband suddenly stopped the car and announced to his kids that it was now time to have fun. He must have just remembered why they were on vacation. She said that his next step was back into his normal character because he then started the car and drove on to the next destination while returning phone calls from work.

Another loss is that the higher you go in an organization, the fewer friends you have. For example, for several years, I very much enjoyed fishing with an employee who reported to me. We averaged going on a fishing trip every month to one of the nearby lakes. He was one of my best friends at that time. That is, until he no longer reported to me. After he moved to another area at work, he never again invited me for a fishing trip. Similar episodes at work happened enough that I started avoiding close relationships with folks in my organization. And yes, I know there are exceptions.

Peer managers are usually friendly out of professional courtesy, but they are also your competitors; therefore, they are rarely true friends. On the other hand, Nonsupervisory workers seem to develop family-like relationships similar to the way soldiers do. Therefore, I concluded that it is better for managers to develop close relationships outside of the workplace.

Jerkitude can Creep Up on you

The person who experiences greatness must have a feeling for the myth he is in. He must reflect what is projected upon him. And he must have a strong sense of the sardonic. This is what uncouples him from belief in his own pretensions. (Dune)

As you reach the top of an organization (without becoming a jerk), you will still find maintaining your non-jerk status to be particularly challenging. This is because the top guy's special treatment from everyone around him tends to turn him into a more profound jerk. The further up he goes in an organization, the more "kowtow-ing to the boss," turns into a coronation and worship of the king. Any person who receives that adoration is quite naturally going to feel superior. It is a short step from feeling superior to acting superior, and acting superior is one of the typical characteristics of a jerk.

As American social reformer, abolitionist, orator, writer, and statesman Fredrick Douglass said, **"The problem with a self-made man is that he ends up worshiping his maker."** Doctors have a par-ticularly difficult time with this issue. Doctors can easily have a god complex because we want doctors to be gods. We want them to be able to defy the very cause of illness. So, we obediently do whatever our omniscient doctor says.

As doctors bask in this exalted light, it is easy to see why they have a high divorce rate. It is hard for physicians to switch out of that role when they get home. A Johns Hopkins study concluded that psychiatrists and surgeons have an especially higher risk of divorce than medical colleagues in other fields.

The same is true for "omnipotent" presidents of corpora-tions. No one ever questions their opinion at work. As an executive becomes accustomed to the work environment, it is easy to imagine that he believes that something must be wrong with spouses who question their obvious "perfection." After all, isn't the spouse living with, serving, and having the honor of raising the king's progeny? We can apply the same logic to attorneys and politicians. The nature of their jobs, status, big money, and lifestyles can quickly pull some-one into inadvertent mega jerkiness.

Some of us learn from other people's mistakes. But, unfortu-nately, the rest of us have to be the "other people." As part of the "other people," I made numerous career mistakes during my working life. As I look back on those mistakes, I find myself wishing I had stumbled upon some of the tips in this book so that I might have avoided all the regrets that came with those mistakes. Of course, I am not saying that if I had read this book, I would have become a corporate chief executive somewhere. But I am saying that I would have reached the end of my corporate career with fewer regrets.

From a career success standpoint, I may not have been any better off at all due to the second reason I have put together the list of tips in this book. That second reason is that so many of my friends ended their careers bitter toward their employers because they never achieved the level of corporate responsibility they felt capable of and deserved. If that group had read this book and realized what they should have done along the way to achieve that level of responsibility, they just might find themselves trading bitterness for pride. Their personal integrity prevented them from actions that could have helped their careers. As the founder of Vanguard, Jack Bogle said, "**If they can take your integrity away from you, it's not integrity.**" Finishing a career without ever compromising your integrity represents a career to be proud of.

Personally, I kept thinking that if I did what was best for the company, I would be noticed -success, fame, and fortune would follow. However, by the time I learned that getting ahead sometimes required actions counter to the business's best interest, I was too old to compete. I had missed the boat. Would I have taken the path to success if I had known what it required at the time? I don't know. I certainly know that I have worked with so many employees who were simply putting the company's interest first in everything they did. They failed to include the implication to their career when taking a position or action. Some of them are disappointed that they did not end up higher on the management chain. I hope they read this book.

Choices

Managers must face that ultimate internal question: **to succumb to complete opportunism or loose the chance to advance.**

There are times when you will need to choose whether to do the right thing for the company or to do the right thing for yourself. That choice is one of being a good steward of the company or a jerk. If you choose to be a jerk, you will have a greater chance of advancing in the company.

You might be saying, "I will be a jerk today, but a good manager when I get to the top." That rarely happens. Once you establish the pattern of being a jerk, it becomes second nature. In fact, as you move further up an organization, it becomes amazingly easy also to rationalize the godlike treatment you are receiving. This special treatment reinforces the ease of maintaining the attributes of a jerk.

This was certainly true for me. I had become a jerk, more because of my position than self-serving actions. It is difficult to keep from feeling superior if everyone around you reports to you. You "are" everyone's superior in the eyes of the company. Everyone is even treating you as if you are superior. And I can personally attest to the fact that feeling superior is an exceptionally good feeling. That feeling is addictive. It took someone who cared about me to steal that feeling from me. I am in his debt today for making me a better person. But I still hate his guts. (Couldn't resist that.)

Summary

Big companies are not living, breathing entities with a brain of their own. Big companies are a group of individuals who each have their own ideas and opinions. It always bothered me when I would hear someone say that IBM says or does something or other. What they should have said was that someone at IBM said or did something. At IBM and most other companies, the ideas and opinions were just as varied as the people. Of course, companies have a culture and general philosophy, but that is about all you can relate concerning "company" positions.

The individuals managing companies have personalities and sensitivities that can become fundamental weaknesses to an organization. An astute person easily exploits those weaknesses. For example, it is simply human nature to have an ego. If you feed the bosses' ego, you have a better chance of reward. You have a better chance to move up. Unfortunately, there are times when feeding those weaknesses can be contrary to the company's best interest. That's the reality in every corporate environment.

To rise to the top, you have to be qualified, which includes having the right personal attributes for the job. To rise to the top, you have to be able to do your job well so that you can become a candidate for management. To rise to the top, you have to be a good manager, undoubtedly requiring much study and personal development. To rise to the top, you have to practice a level of work commitment that may put personal and family relationships at risk. To rise to the top, you will also have to consider your personal best interests in every action and decision you make.

It is that last item that can make you into a jerk. The culture and practices in corporations that determine who receives promotions favor individuals who are cunning and self-serving. The treatment managers receive in executive positions also reinforces the behavior often associated with a narcissistic person. There is also an addictive nature to the power given to top managers in a corporation. This does not mean that top managers are not competent managers, far from it. They must be competent to achieve that level. They are, however, almost always ultimately focused on themselves. Maybe not every single one, but as a category, the average senior manager is a jerk. I enjoyed seeing a recent quote from Ferdinand Piech, who became a remarkably successful head of Volkswagen. He was asked what it took to be successful. His reply was **"to be born right and disregard entirely the humanity of others."** What would you call Piech?

In my first professional job, I found myself mystified by the observation that many middle-level managers and non-managers seemed to be far more capable contributors to the company than the top executives. I now realize that those very competent employees, either knowingly or unknowingly, put integrity, their personal life, and the organization's good above their career. I am proud to have known them.

AFTERWORD

A Better Way

Typically, managers become jerks on the way to the top. By contrast, when a manager reaches the top by unconventional methods, something special can happen. An example is from the IBM of old. According to the popular book "Big Blue," Thomas Watson Sr., who founded IBM, was an excellent salesmen but, practiced a callous approach, both with his customers and his employees. However, an interesting and unique cultural shift began happening when he turned the company over to his son, Thomas Watson Jr. Thomas Jr. was a humble visionary who instilled a culture of respect that extended to customers and employees. As a result, the company flourished under his style of leadership.

I joined IBM in 1980, which may have been the peak of its glory days. I had worked at three other big companies before IBM and was taken aback by the contrast in management philosophy between IBM and other companies. The team-oriented environment was not only a great place to work, but it also achieved outstanding results. However, a lesson for me was to see how perishable that competitive edge was. As IBM began backing away from all the employee-centric programs, employees stopped putting in the extra effort. Perhaps Tom Watson Jr. stepping down, was not the only cause for changes in IBM but it does seem to fit the timeline of his influence.

Since I often traveled during the normal workweek, I frequently went into the office at IBM on Saturday mornings to catch up on paperwork. Early in my career, I noticed that the parking lots were almost full on a typical Saturday. Then one particular Saturday, I noticed a drastic difference. I had been on assignment at a distant location for three years, and my first weekend back decided to drop by the office on Saturday morning. As I drove my car into one of the main parking lots, I noticed that it was totally empty. That was a sad day for me. The company had lost its edge.

The factors that influence management selection and motivation at most US companies continue to encourage choices often detrimental to the long-term health of a corporation. Unfortunately, the measurement and reward system for top executives exaggerates that effect by looking exclusively at quarterly results instead of long-term success.

Notwithstanding the power motive, money dominates the incentive for reaching the top of a company. The Economist magazine points out that the average CEO in the U.S. makes 350 times the wage of the hourly worker. Their data shows that this is also several times the average in European countries. In England, the average is 75 times the hourly worker. The argument has been, that in the U.S. there are very few of these special people and they must be highly rewarded. I have known many executive-level managers, including well-known names like Jack Welch. I have met some who were very good at their job. I have never met one who was "special." In fact, in every company where I have worked, I could name 100 people equally capable of being the CEO.

It is easy to see how this ridiculously high CEO salary in the U.S. encourages and motivates the adoption of a "do anything to advance" attitude for aspiring executives. This avarice incentive often overwhelms judgment and actions that might be in the company's best interest. It causes managers to place self-interest above all other considerations and can cause the manager to become a real jerk.

A root cause of the U.S. salary disparity is the result of the business philosophy of companies' commitment to maximizing **shareholder value**. Executives are compensated massively with stock options and bonuses to ensure their focus on increasing shareholder value at the expense of everything else. Instead of using profits for expansion and development, they buy back company stock to add shareholder value. They likewise, structure bonus incentives for management based exclusively on profits that drive stock value. As a result, customers, employees, the environment, and society as a whole all take a back seat. Although the results can be soaring short-term profits, employee salaries stagnate, and corporate life expectancy declines. The company's life expectancy declines because little or no consideration is given to long-term growth and longevity.

A popular alternative to maximizing shareholder value supported by Klaus Schwab, Executive Chairman, World Economic Forum, is called **stakeholder capitalism**. The premise is that companies should focus on meeting the needs of all stakeholders: customers, employees, partners, the community, and society. I agree that a stakeholder board of directors would be ideal. However, I fear that a corporate focus on all stakeholders would result in constant conflicts between what is best for each of the stakeholders. Those conflicts could lead to consternation and decision delays that can bring an organization to its knees as it loses critical opportunities.

A better alternative is the simpler **customer-focused capitalism** or what Peter Drucker called the "True North" for a corporation. The overriding goal of the company is to create customers. Creating customers is the result of providing exceptional value in meeting their needs. That value is the basis for generating benefits for all the stakeholders, including stockholders. Of course, a company cannot overlook the requirements of all stakeholders, but it is the customers who must receive the highest priority.

So, if this is a reasonably obvious better philosophy to follow for managing a business, how do you make that happen? I don't know. I do know that companies who seem to follow that strategy have thrived (Amazon, Facebook, Google, Microsoft, Dell, Tesla). An interesting factor common to these enormously successful customer focused companies is that the person at the top during their phenomenal growth was the company's founder. He was not the jerk who had clawed his way to the top through self-serving actions. He was also singularly focused on providing the best solution for the needs of the customer. They were customer-focused first, with confidence that profits would follow.

Another example contrasting the norm for current U.S. companies is the large companies founded by a family and are still guided by the family. These companies seem to have more sense of permanence than similar companies directed by professional managers.

Microsoft is also a good example of shrewd planning and customer focused. In the early days of the PC business there were a number of providers for office software. They were all rather costly but essential to have. Microsoft, by contrast, practically gave their versions away. In many cases, their software came with the initial operating system. They had accurately recognized that eventually everyone would need the same software. By becoming that standard, they could lock in that segment for the long term. At that time their software was adequate, but inferior to some of the other providers. (Lotus 123 vs Excel, Freelance vs Power Point, Word Perfect vs Word). Today, those competitors are largely memories for old PC nerds like me. And now, that "standard" office software has become an essential, but expensive annual payment to Microsoft.

This example is the exception because so many of today's companies are focused instead on short-term profits first, with customer solutions as a means to the desired results. I pointed out the unique team environment in the IBM of old. Because of their parallel path for career advancement, non-managers could have just as nice of an office and make just as much money as higher-level managers. I attribute their downward slide to the abandonment of that practice along with their move toward shareholder focus.

Companies can change. The best example is when a shareholder focused company is bought by a customer focused company. This actually happens frequently as the successful customer focused companies accumulate the funds for growing by acquisition. As a result, many times a mediocre company is turned around by simply changing the culture - along with key management.

But is it possible for a current company to change to customer focus without the type of wholesale shake-up involved in a take-over? I hope so because there seems to be **many companies that could use an overhaul.**

So, where would you start with that overhaul? One step would be to disconnect management compensation from short-term profits and stock performance. Another would be to stop paying executives ridiculously high salaries. So, how would you do either of those? How could you change a company from shareholder focused to customer focused? Who is it that would say to executives: "Oh, by the way, you now make a fraction of what you were making because we are changing philosophy?" One problem with saying that, is that the person who has to say it is the Chairman of the Board, who may also be the President with the ridiculous compensation. Nevertheless, the fact that a condition exists in corporate America that can harm the company's health, means that corporations must make changes. The following are a few logical points to consider:

The top of the company is a sensible place to start for aligning the company's interests with the interests of employees. Unfortunately, the top will undoubtedly be the most difficult arena to effect change because those who can make the needed changes will be affected. It is akin to asking Congress to adopt term limits. Why would a member of Congress favor a rule that would put him out of a job? Nevertheless, a conscientious and sincere corporate leader should consider this condition and possible remedies. I don't doubt that their personal perspective would yield even more suggestions.

Taking a further look at the unusually high executive compensation in the U.S., we notice that the board of directors usually sets executive pay rates. As I look at the makeup of executive boards, I am often confused. Most of the boards seem to be made up of high-profile people who are members of so many other boards that they could not possibly have any meaningful time to dedicate to the intricacies of any particular company. In addition, they often seem to have no background that would qualify them for making strategic decisions on the type of businesses where they are board members. This fact makes it even easier for a strong CEO (who often serves as both CEO and Chairman of the board) to become almost autonomous in making strategic decisions.

Having the CEO and chairman positions combined guarantees a myopic strategy and diminishes any independent oversight of management. Moreover, having the board made up of token celebrities further enables the dysfunctional board, as few are qualified to challenge the company's management. This situation would have to change before a more strategic and sustainable vision for companies could emerge.

Therefore, the selection and self-perpetuating nature of the board of directors is an area to be addressed. Although the stockholders theoretically elect the board, it is essentially the board that names the candidates, resulting in a stacked board. As a result, stockholders rarely have meaningful choices. Although the primary purpose of a company is to provide a return for the investors, there must also be a recognition of the employee contribution in that effort. Therefore, an ideal board would be made up of stakeholders intimately familiar with the business and motivated by the best interest in the company's long-term viability. Two groups immediately surface as stakeholders, stockholders, and employees. Yes, I have already questioned stakeholder capitalism, but having stakeholders other than shareholders has merit.

Employees are familiar with the business and motivated by the long-term viability of the company. Stockholders may or may not be familiar with the business, but certainly have a motivation for the business's profitability and viability. Of course, stockholders come and go based on investment goals which tends to force a focus on the short term. That fact, which would hinder stockholder involvement when considering an organization's long-term goals, would need to be balanced by those motivated to ensure long-term viability.

Fixing irrational executive compensation would be another hurdle. It might be helpful to understand how we got here and why the U.S. is so much different from other advanced nations. Of course, as noted, the board sets executive compensation. I am confident that the board would be surprised to discover how few executives would leave the company if their pay were less.

A cynical view might conclude that the government may solve this problem. As we continue to print money and spend, taxes must increase. A logical move would be to return to the Eisenhower tax rates that topped out at 91% for high incomes. This would reduce the advantage of gargantuan salaries but does not address the root cause. The root cause seems to be that senior executives have a powerful influence over setting their own compensation. It would take a different corporate structure for that to change.

In addition to changes in the directing boards, a different process for selecting management could help prevent the conflict between candidates who are faced with choices that improve their personal standing versus choices in the company's best interest. In most companies today, the next level of management selects the person he wants. This has become something of a "good old boy" process that naturally encourages the behavior of aspiring candidates based on how their boss might perceive them. The question then, is how to align personal motivation with company interest. And, of course, that depends on what the company's best interests are determined to be. If it is short-term results, then nothing changes. If it is long-term viability and growth, then something must change. Of course, we could add other stakeholder interests as well in that list of company goals.

The military uses an interesting process designed to address some of this conflict. Promotions in the military are most often the result of the consensus of a review board. The review board bases the selections on performance and experience factors that continue to be refined for ensuring impartial and best choices. However, I am guessing that rank in that review board could still be a complicating factor.

A useful tool for ensuring better management selections is to conduct annual employee surveys, which can be a good method for improving management effectiveness. Good surveys are often long and comprehensive, soliciting employee feedback on many company programs and issues. However, the most significant value is the anonymous feedback on the perceived performance of management. At the IBM of old, it was common for a manager who received a poor survey to be taken out of management. Fortunately, because of IBM's parallel career structure, moving out of management rarely meant a demotion; instead, it was usually a simple job change. Of course, the survey results must be considered as only one aspect of management effectiveness. Departmental results are certainly the most important factor.

These changes will be difficult to implement for many companies. However, recognizing the complexity of effecting real change in a corporation to improve the quality of management should not dissuade the effort. It is essential to recognize that the quality of management in a company is the fundamental requirement for creating a successful enterprise. They must be motivated to act in the best interest of the company. Instead of a reward system dependent on job level, the reward should depend on corporate success. The corporate success would need to include multiple factors that reflect the goals of the corporation. Such a system would reward team effort and consensus decisions, which are essential keys to successful corporations.

To summarize then, if you want to keep from having a jerk at the top of your company, switch to a customer focused strategy, shake up your board by adding experts, pay your executives a good salary, not based on quarterly results, reduce the pay difference between employees and management, and let employees have a say in management choices. How do you make such fundamental changes? Sorry, I don't know. I hope you have an idea.